f.92

14 Oct

f-92

MODERN MONTESSORI AT HOME II

A Creative Teaching Guide
for Parents of Children
10 through 12 Years of Age

HEIDI ANNE SPIETZ

American Montessori Consulting
Rossmoor, California

i

ABOUT THE AUTHOR

Heidi Anne Spietz, author of "Montessori at Home",
"Modern Montessori at Home", and "Modern Mont
at Home II" holds a B.Sc. degree from REX Universi
New York, Albany and a diploma in Montessori trai
In 1979 she was awarded but declined because of oth
commitments, the prestigious CORO award. She h
general memberships in both the American Montess
Society and Association Montessori Internationale,
lands Chapter. She is well acquainted with how the
tessori method is used in the United States and in
because she received her training from London, En
She has taught at private schools in the United Sta
concurrently managing her own successful tutorin
ness for the past six years.

Library of Congress Cataloging-in-Publication Data
Spietz, Heidi Anne,
Modern Montessori at home II: a creative teaching guide for parents of children 10 through 12 years of age / Heidi Anne Spietz.
p. cm.
Includes bibliographical references (p.) and index.
ISBN 0-929487-10-9 : $9.95
1. Montessori method of education. 2. Home schooling - - United States. I. title. II. title : Modern Montessori at home 2.
LB775. M8S757 1990
649'.68 - - dc20

                                        90-834
                                        CIP

This book is dedicated to my family members, Carl, Frances and Susan. I thank them for their love and encouragement. A special thanks goes to my mother, Frances, for her artistic input into the making of this book.

Thanks also to Dr. Kazan and Dr. Edwin Brosbe, of California State University, Long Beach. They made the study of microbiology fascinating and challenging for their students. I think of them often when I present science and health lessons to my students and hope that I have inspired them in the way that they inspired their students.

I also owe much to Mr. Wellington and Mrs. Louise Blake of East Middle School of Downey, California. They made learning literature and grammar fascinating as well as meaningful.

A very special thanks to the people of Happy One Hour Photo of Seal Beach, California for their superb job with the photography, and to the owners and staff of Plaza Insta Print of Los Alamitos, California for the manufacturing of this book. Cover picture courtesy of The Printers Shopper, 111 Press Lane, Chula Vista, California 92010.

Finally, I feel much gratitude for the students I have come in contact with during the past seven years. Through them I have seen the magic of Maria Montessori's principles at work.

TABLE OF CONTENTS

Chapter	Page

CREATIVE LESSON PLANNING
CHAPTER I

Maria Montessori's dream of educating a generation of normalized children is still a hope shared by
many enlightened educators from every corner of the
world. Montessori realized that peace and harmony
could only be achieved by allowing children to develop
in an environment which provided the sustenance and
encouragement so needed for normal development.
She further contended that because some adults stifle
independent thinking and actions through unconscious
manipulations or through domination, some children
feel as though they are less important and useful than
the adults they so admire. Consequently, these children
feel inhibited, self-conscious and possibly resentful.

It is therefore the role of educators and teachers to
see that this next generation receive as much positive
reinforcement and encouragement in their attempts at
mastering new concepts as possible. For the amount of
global concerns which will affect this generation of
children is a little overwhelming. If we do not take the
time to educate these children properly, aren't we fail-
ing them as well as future generations to come? Therefore, we must realize the need to include our children as
co-caretakers of the earth; we must encourage them to
become involved citizens now while they are young.

Maria Montessori realized that the needs of older
children greatly differ from the younger ones. Thus, the
role of the teacher/parent who acts as "presenter" must
likewise change. Although the older child still needs the
time to make the discoveries and spontaneous explo-
sions which are essential components of the learning
process, his need for direction at this stage of develop-

ment is heightened. Unfortunately, this need for direction is sometimes misinterpreted by the presenter. Some presenters find it tempting to become too involved in helping the child master a concept. Consequently, they interfere by completing a task instead of allowing the child to complete the task on his own.

For example, the presenter feels uneasy as he watches the child awkwardly attempt to draw the continents on the posterboard, so he may inhibit the child's further attempts by insisting that the child watch as the presenter completes the drawing. This only reinforces the child's doubts about his drawing ability and discourages his curiosity about the continent involved.

Conversely, a "presenter" who provides *direction* and *guidance* **when requested** helps the child to mature into a self-actualized human being. She realizes that she must allow the child to make the mistakes so that he will learn from his errors. If his work is imperfect she will praise the outstanding aspects of his work while suggesting that he explore additional activities which will help him to learn more from his errors. For example, if a child writes a three page paper about the musical composers of the Renaissance period but fails to mention Palestrina's work, then one would assume that the child did not do much research. However, if the composition is organized and interesting the "presenter" will want to praise the child for these accomplishments. Suggestions as to where the child may have gone to do additional research about the composers of this period would also be given. Therefore, the child learns about various reference materials available to him. His self-esteem remains undamaged, and because the "presenter" was basically positive about the report, the child will be open to further learning.

Creative Lesson Planning

The use of creative lesson planning will help you to develop stimulating learning exercises for your child or children. Creative lesson planning involves defining the objective to be taught, consideration of the child's ability to appreciate the concept to be learned, allocating the appropriate amount of time needed for the presentation and practice period, preparation of the lesson and allowing for a certain amount of flexibility during the learning session.

Children in the 10-12 age bracket often challenge the presenter's knowledge. This is very natural. However, some presenters feel uncomfortable when children question their expertise in the different areas of study. The presenter need not feel that he must have all the answers to the multitude of questions that children pose. The presenter can't possibly conceive of all the questions which might arise during the learning sessions. However, a thorough knowledge of the subject presented is a necessity. The presenter must feel confident that he has mastered the "basics" of whatever he is presenting. If he is uncertain of the concepts involved, he may feel unable to give a clear presentation to the child or children. Many children are quite perceptive and they readily know when we are bluffing or quite confident about the subject matter which is being presented.

This fact is well known to educators. Therefore, if you are a teacher who wishes to incorporate some of the ideas in this book into your lesson plans, the aforementioned probably seems very redundant. However, if you are a parent who wishes to use the ideas presented in this book to either supplement your child's school work or home learning, keep in mind that your preparation will have a direct bearing on whether your presentations are successful or not.

Planning the Presentation

Spend time researching the topic you will be presenting. If you are planning to present a lesson on comparative art of a given period, i.e. Renaissance/Baroque period, you may want to borrow some books about art history from your local library. If you are fortunate enough to have an art museum close by, stop in for a visit. Be sure to have a pencil and notebook handy so that you can take notes about the difference in the paintings, i.e. analyzing the composition, styles used, techniques applied, and so on. Moreover, you will want to obtain postcard reproductions of the famous paintings so that you can refer to them during your presentations. You may have to spend a little time writing to the owners of various museum bookshops to inquire as to the availability and cost of the postcards. Moreover, a little legwork will be involved as you visit the various art galleries to learn more about the art world in general. Don't be afraid to ask questions! Your discussions with the connoisseurs of art will be enlightening. You may even decide to present a comparative lesson involving the Baroque period with Modern Art.

Defining the Objective

Consider what you want your child to gain from your presentations. For example, if your goal is to help your child learn the relationship of one continent to another you will first need to determine if your child is able to recognize and give appropriate directions on a smaller scale. Therefore, exercises like the Geography/Community Road Game help your child learn to identify different streets by their geographical location. Once he can identify whether buildings and streets are northeast, southwest or northwest from each other, he will readily grasp the geographical locations of the continents.

If your child's sentences are fragmented or run together then you must first determine if he can identify the subject and verb pattern of a sentence. Next, ascertain if he readily recognizes the different parts of speech in a sentence. If he seems uncertain, than you may want to encourage your child to first diagram simple sentences. After you feel that he is confident in this task than you will want to encourage him to diagram complex sentences. From these diagraming exercises your child will learn to appreciate the structure and function that the sentence serves. Another stimulating and rewarding exercise called the Grammar Bingo Game also reinforces parts of speech recognition in a relaxed atmosphere.

Whenever possible, encourage your child to become involved in the construction of the games and other learning activities mentioned throughout this book. Maria Montessori recognized that children of all ages learn by doing. Thus, your child absorbs knowledge from these "hands-on" experiences as well as by participating in the learning activities.

Considering Your Child's Ability

It is essential that you take the time to consider just how familiar your child is with the subject matter being presented as well as his ability to grasp the concept which is being presented. Children do learn at different rates. For example, if your child is experiencing difficulty in the area of English composition you may want to consider obtaining a copy of **Modern Montessori at Home: A Creative Teaching Guide for Parents of Children Six through Nine Years of Age.** A complete introduction to writing simple sentences as well as beginning compositions is presented in this book. Although this book is designed for children six through nine years of age, older children benefit from the exercises presented in this book too!

Never push your child to absorb concepts quickly. He needs to learn the concepts at his own pace. Allow him the freedom to make errors and learn from these mistakes that he makes. When he has grasped the concept presented he will feel confident and ready to move on to mastering yet another new concept.

Flexible Lesson Planning

As you plan your lesson, consider the element of time. First, rehearse the presentation. You will discover if you have left certain steps out. Moreover, by rehearsing the presentation you can determine if portions of the lesson seem nebulous. Remember, if parts of the presentation seem confusing to you, they will be equally so for your child. Thus, this rehearsal time gives you an ideal opportunity to smooth over those rough spots. Futhermore, you will gain confidence from reviewing the material to be presented. The material will seem more solidified in your mind and you will feel more relaxed as you present the lesson to your child.

I know from experience just how important the rehearsal time actually is. I remember when I first started to substitute teach. I never knew what grade I would be asked to teach; therefore, I knew that there would be some lesson plans left by the primary teacher which would be unfamiliar to me. Usually, this primary teacher left specific directions as to how she wanted this lesson presented, but because I had not had the opportunity to rehearse the presentation, I never felt completely relaxed. However, when I am the primary teacher, I plan the lesson and *I* have the opportunity to rehearse the material beforehand.

If you are an elementary teacher using this book as a tool to help you incorporate some of Montessori's principles into your classroom you know how important flexible lesson planning really is. Sometimes a student will ask a fascinating question and you realize that the answer to this question will not only satisfy the student's curiosity but will lend itself to a stimulating classroom discussion as well. A rigid time schedule, therefore, is not always conducive to learning. Realizing this, you probably already allow some time for a question and answer period.

If you are a parent who is either teaching your child at home or using this book as a supplement to your child's learning program, incorporate flexible lesson planning into your learning program. Be aware that your child may need to take extra time to review a concept that was presented during a previous learning session before he can proceed with the lesson at hand. Montessori encouraged this review time. She realized also that sometimes a child will be so fascinated with a concept that was presented during a previous session that he may wish to continue working with it. This should not be discouraged. However, if a child signals to you that he is bored and wants to move on, do so. Remember, you are not catering to his needs. Rather, you are becoming sensitive to the intellectual stimuli needed to help him on his path towards becoming a self-actualized human being.

Montessori for Today

As parents and teachers we have the responsibility to provide this next generation with educational experiences which will prove to be stimulating. The vast global concerns which afflict society today will not disappear overnight. The solutions to many problems which perplex mankind will undoubtedly come about through the innovative thinking of the next generation. Thus, we must teach them as much as possible about the world around them. They must not be complacent and uncaring about what is happening in third world countries. Rather, they must be taught about people from every corner of the world. Moreover, they must learn how to protect the environment not only for themselves but for mankind.

The lessons in this book will help you to provide varied educational experiences which will help your child see the interrelationships between the various academic disciplines. He will see how art, music and literature reflect a certain historical period. He will see how the work of the coral affects the calcium cycle and how natural and unnatural disasters, i.e. pollution disrupt this cycle. Your child will discover the relationship of cellular growth to proper nutrition. He will also learn the relationship of disease to poor eating habits. As he studies about the different decades in American history, he learns to communicate his findings by giving oral reports, constructing graphs and exploring a given historical event or personality through essay. As he learns more about mankind he learns more about himself. He sees that his decisions can and do make a difference. He discovers the importance of becoming an involved citizen. As a parent or teacher, you have the satisfaction of knowing that you are integral ingredient in helping this child develop into an educated, environmentally aware pre-teen!

LESSONS IN SCIENCE FOR FIFTH, SIXTH AND SEVENTH GRADERS
CHAPTER II

Traditionally, our children have received fragmented learning in "each" of the academic subjects. Math, reading, biology, geography and the like have been presented in a vacuum. Fortunately, during the past decade, public and private schools have re-examined their curricula and have integrated more of an interdisciplinary approach into lesson planning.

As a parent, you can insure that your child receives an in-depth, examination of how the disciplines interrelate. By properly preparing the learning environment, you create the atmosphere for self-discovery and exploration. As your child sees the relationship of one discipline to another, he learns more about the world and his place in it.

Maria Montessori often spoke and even wrote about the work of the coral. In fact, she paralleled the cosmic work of the coral to the unique work that each person is destined to accomplish. By introducing the task of the coral during the first part of this science lesson, your child will begin to see the myriad of factors which contribute to its existence. He will discover that many components make up the whole. By presenting this lesson on the coral, your child will see how biology, geology, microbiology and other disciplines relate to each other. Thus, studying a topic presented in one scientific discipline will pose additional questions which will be answered by studying related disciplines.

The Fascinating World of the Coral

Coral reefs are magnificent to look at. If you have a set of encyclopedias with colored pictures of coral reefs or copies of *National Geographic* with articles and pictures about reefs handy, you will want to encourage your child to take a peek at these breathtaking works of nature. Encourage your child to read as much as possible about coral reefs, so that he will have some appreciation of what the two of you will be discussing.

Next, explain that the corals are probably "the" most important animal that can be found on the reefs. Their existence has encouraged other life forms to settle on the reefs as well. The reefs provide protection for many forms of aquatic life. The bivalve molluscs and sponges are just two of many species that find refuge there. The corals, then, are an integral part of the microcosm that can be found in this tropical habitat.

Continue by explaining that corals come from minute marine animals called coral polyps. The polyp hatches from an egg. Once in its larva stage of development, it slowly floats away and falls until its rests on a section of the reef. The polyp uses available calcium and carbonate from the surrounding water to create a protective skeleton. This hard skeleton also allows the coral to attach itself to its final resting place. When the coral dies, his skeleton remains behind and becomes part of the coral reef.

The coral reef is built by the accumulation of skeletons from dead corals plus the remains of other aquatic life forms that make up this magnificent microcosm. Living polyps attach themselves to the skeletal remains. Thus, the reef formation is an ongoing process.

Emphasize during this lesson that favorable conditions promote the proliferation of life forms, while negative conditions interfere or discourage such growth. The coral polyp is no exception to this truism. With a world map or globe close at hand, show your child that coral reef formation is restricted to tropical and subtropical latitudes. The temperature requirements are very specific. Growth flourishes in temperatures above 74°F. You may want to point out on the globe or world map that most reefs will be located on the eastern coasts of the continents. Explain, that the eastern coasts receive warmer waters, while the western coasts receive the colder waters from the North and South Poles. Now, direct your child's attention to Reef Formation Chart A. Explain that there are three distinctive types of coral reefs. They are as follows: 1) the barrier reefs which can be found on the outer regions of the continental shelves, 2) the fringing reefs which are located along the outer edges of the coastlines and 3) atolls which arise from the floor of the ocean. The atolls are found capping undersea mountains.

The calcareous algae are thought to be a prime contributor to the construction of the coral reef. They secrete a tough chalky crystal which eventually contributes to the rubble that is called "home" to the filamentous algae. These filamentous algae in turn use photosynthesis to capture energy that will be used by other predators. (A complete discussion of photosynthesis will be given later). At this point, explain to your child that "photosynthesis" is a process whereby green plants and some algae use light to make food for themselves, and, indirectly, for their consumers.

Sponges, bryozoa, the gastropod, and bivalve molluscs are just some of the other organisms that contribute to the building of the coral reef. Like the coral polyp, the calcium carbonate deposits from these aquatic organisms contributes to the growth of the reef. The balance of life on the coral reefs also depends on the relationship that the organisms have with one another.

Discuss with your child how a peaceful coexistence benefits all members of the aquatic community. Emphasize that some corals eat during the night while others feed during the daylight hours. Other aquatic

11

REEF FORMATION
CHART A
REEF TYPES

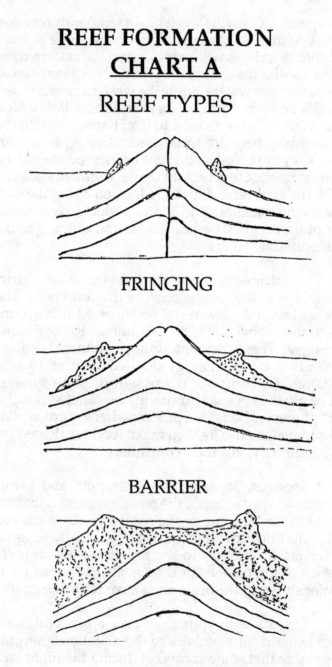

FRINGING

BARRIER

ATOLL

life, like certain species of fish, also differ in their eating patterns. Some prefer to eat when the tidal and current conditions are at a given level. This give and take relationship results in harmony within this marine community.

Destructive factors, unfortunately, interfere with the growth of the coral reef. Some factors are quite natural. Others are a result of man's interference. For example, if the water becomes too polluted by oil, toxic chemicals, or from other forms of pollution, the algae polyps die. Remind your child that the algae polyps are dependent upon adequate sunlight. Without this sunlight photosynthesis cannot occur.

The coral needs an ample amount of salt to insure its survival. Natural factors like a turbulent storm which dilutes salt water will result in coral polyp death. Thus, we see that a change in the chemical consistency of the water will tip the balance against coral survival.

Some sponges, too, tend to destroy rather than contribute to the formation of the coral reef. The Boring Sea-Urchin bores holes through the coral polyps. However, the sponge is not the sole destroyer of the reef. His companion, the Crown-of-thorns Starfish is also thought to prey upon the corals.

During the 1960's, the Crown-of-thorns began invading an area in the northeast corner of Australia, known as the Great Barrier Reef. This predator, unfortunately, is known to eat the fleshy part of the coral while leaving the coral skeleton behind. Unhappily, the Crown-of-thorns continues to prey on the corals at present. Some researchers have found, however, that the Crown-of-thorns attacks are sporadic and that the untouched coral polyps are recolonizing the reefs.

Learning about – C H O N – The Elements of Life

All living aerobic organisms need carbon (C), hydrogen (H), oxygen (O), and nitrogen (N) for their existence. Elementary chemistry can easily be introduced to your child if you use movable models for your presentations. Models for using the movable alphabet, pictured in **Montessori at Home** and phonics models, pictured in **Modern Montessori at Home** were used to help children appreciate and understand the functions of letters and sounds. These models helped the children see the association of letters and sounds to reading and spelling. Models can also be used to help children see how carbon, hydrogen, oxygen and nitrogen unite to form usable substances.

Using one sheet of blue construction paper, one sheet of gray construction paper, one sheet of black construction paper and one sheet of white construction paper, instruct your child to draw and cut several circles, each measuring a diameter of three inches. Next, using one sheet of white construction paper, ask your child to draw and cut thin rectangular squares, each measuring approximately 1/4" x 3" in length.

C	H	O	N
Black	White	Blue	Gray

Explain that the long rectangular squares will be used as arms to connect the circles. Designate the blue circles as oxygen (O) atoms, the gray circles as nitrogen (N) atoms, the white circles as hydrogen (H) atoms and the black circles as carbon (C) atoms. (See page 17 for an example of how the atoms are linked together.)

Explain to your child that carbon has four arms. Therefore, he will need to glue four arms which will extend from the black circle. Using a clock as a guide, he may want to glue one arm at the 12 o'clock position, one arm at the 3 o'clock, one arm at the 6 o'clock position and one arm at the 9 o'clock position (-●-). Instruct your child to make some of the carbon atoms as follows (-●-). In these models the arms are horizontal so that the arms can easily be joined with other atoms.

Next, explain that hydrogen has one arm. Thus, your child will need to glue only one long rectangular arm to the white circle. The blue circle which represents oxygen, should have two arms extending from it. Finally, explain that nitrogen should have three arms extending from it.

Your child may have learned at school or through the media that H_2O represents water. Illustrate with the models that oxygen combines with two atoms of hydrogen. Next, impress upon your child that oxygen has two arms (-⊘-). Now, ask your child to connect one of the hydrogen atoms to the oxygen atom by overlapping the arms (O—⊘). He should now see that the oxygen atom still has one arm that is free. Next, ask him to connect another hydrogen atom to the oxygen atom. He will see that the two arms overlap, thus, a connection is made. (O—⊘   —O) becomes (O—⊘—O). Later, once you are certain that your child appreciates the significance of the arms, explain that in actuality the hydrogen atoms are located on one side of the oxygen atom 104.5° apart (⚭).

Carbon dioxide, written as CO_2, can also be demonstrated by using the chemistry models. Ask your child to give you the black circle, designated as carbon, with the arms extended in a horizontal fashion (═●═). Next, ask that he also give you an oxygen atom. Impress upon your child that the arms can be moved from one position to another, so that the connection of the atoms in this model will be very clear. For example, the oxygen atom can be changed from (─⊘─) to (⊘═). Notice that the "amount" of arms on the model has not changed. Only the positioning of these arms has changed. Now, ask your child to join the carbon atom (═●═) with the oxygen atom (═●═ ═⊘ → ═●═⊘).

He now sees that the carbon atom still has two arms that are free. Now, show that by attaching another oxygen atom (⊘═●═⊘) CO_2 has been formed. Once again, when you feel that your child has fully comprehended the significance of the arms show how CO_2 is illustrated in chemistry.

At this point, you may wish to discuss with your child that calcium carbonate, which is utilized by the corals, is also a very intricate component in the formation of the atolls.

CHEMISTRY MODEL A

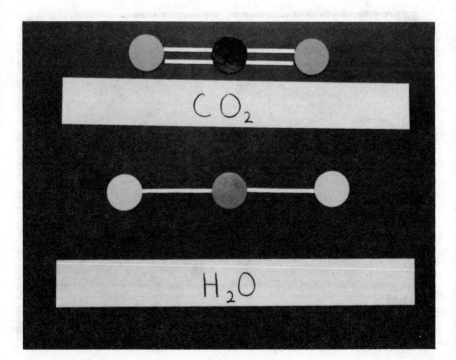

CHEMISTRY MODEL B

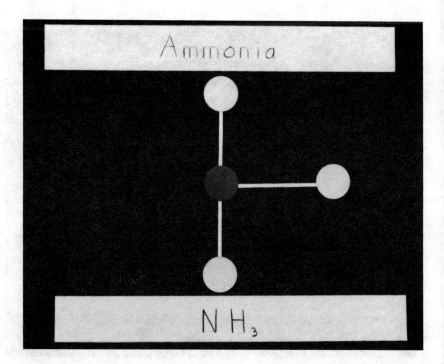

CHEMISTRY MODEL C

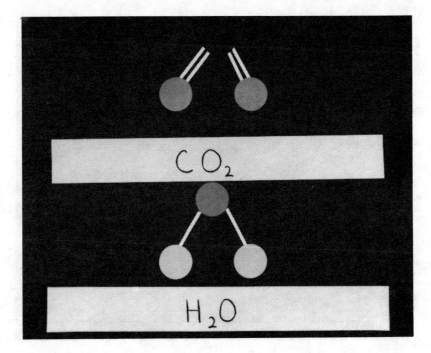

CHEMISTRY MODEL D

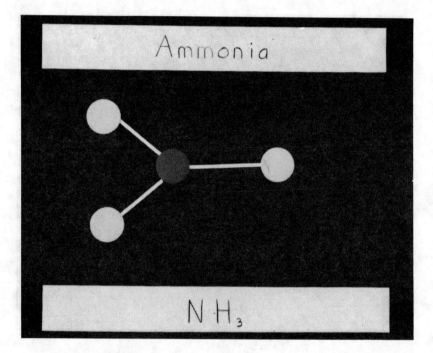

Chemistry in Action – The Ecosystem

Perhaps one of the best ways to illustrate to your child chemistry's role in the environment is to present a lesson covering a relevant topic like "ecology" with him. During this discussion you can refer to CO_2, H_2O and the like. He will further see the relevance of how these chemicals are utilized and recycled in the environment as you explain the chemical applications involved in the study of the ecosystem.

Explain to your child that in the ecosystem there are three types of organisms: producers, consumers and decomposers. The producers fix energy; the consumers use a portion of this fixed energy; and decomposers recycle the remaining organic materials into usable inorganic materials which will later be used by the producers.

Further explain that the producers, like the algae of the coral reef, transform or fix radiant energy from the sun into a complex chemical bond of energy via a process known as "photosynthesis". The algae are responsible for approximately 80% of all photosynthesis, while on land, we see that the green plant does its share to contribute to this important process. Explain to your child that the leaves of the plant contain chlorophyll. The chlorophyll, found in the chloroplast cells of the plant, permits water H_2O, and carbon dioxide, CO_2, from the plant's stomata cells to combine in such a way that "sugar" or "energy" is stored.

Further discuss with your child that the word "photosynthesis" means "putting together by way of light". This process *always* requires the presence of chlorophyll.

The equation for the photosynthesis process is as follows:

$$CO_2 + H_2O + Sunlight \rightarrow (C\,H_2O) + O_2$$

Carbon Dioxide + Water + Sunlight $\rightarrow$ Carbohydrate + Oxygen

The consumers can be separated into two distinct groups. The first level consumer eats producer organisms. Since the producers are plants, phytoplankton and algae, these first level consumers are referred to as "herbivores". Explain that the term "herbivore" means plant eating. The first level consumers, which are usually animals, are often eaten by second level consumers.

The second level consumers may be "herbivores", "carnivores" or "omnivores". Explain that the term "carnivore" refers to eating animals, while the term "omnivore" means consuming both plant and animal products. Thus, a cow grazes on the grass. The grass is the producer and the cow is the first level consumer. You may want to give an additional example. For example, a mouse easts grass. The mouse is then consumed by the weasel. Finally, the weasel may be consumed by the cat. In the latter example, the grass is the producer, and the mouse is the first level consumer, (herbivore). The weasel is the second level consumer, (carnivore), and the cat is the third level consumer (carnivore).

Ask your child to draw a pyramid like the one pictured on page 24. If your child doesn't like to draw, suggest that he cut out pictures from various magazines where aquatic life is illustrated or pictured. His pyramid should show that the producer level has phytoplankton pictured at the base. On the next level, small animals like zooplankton should be pictured. On the third level, plankton consuming fish should be pictured. On the fourth level larger fish should be pictured. On the top level, a shark should be pictured.

Next, discuss with your child how energy is lost at each one of the levels. Although there is a transfer of energy from one organism to another, about 85% is lost at each level. Discuss with your child how the organism must use some of the energy to sustain its life. Moreover, explain that a portion of the energy is used while the organism reproduces itself. Another portion of the energy is left behind as waste material, and it is subsequently used by the decomposer organisms. You may want to discuss at this point that the energy conscious person tries to consume much of his diet at the lower end of the spectrum of this pyramid. Your child may enjoy doing some research on food chains and food webs. Suggest that he write an essay on the structure and function of the food chain. He will gain much understanding about the delicate balance involved in food webs and foods chains from completing this exercise.

As you and your child look at a world map or survey the area on your world globe, explain that two-thirds of the earth is occupied by oceans. Thus, the oceans could play a very important role in feeding the world's population. Obviously, some oceanic areas will always be more productive than others. Areas of upwelling and coastal regions are particularly productive. These areas have the needed nutrients and appropriate amount of light to "fix" energy that can be used by the producers and consumers. Unfortunately, in the open oceanic areas only 2 grams of CO_2 are fixed. Only a fraction of the light enters this area; moreover, there is also a substantial lack of nutrients needed to "fix" the energy.

Conversely, in an upwelling area, the currents meet from two different directions and depths. This creates an upwelling or mixing effect. Nutrients from the lower oceanic regions are then deposited into the upper oceanic layer and fixed by phytoplankton via photosynthesis. Since there is a substantial amount of

MARINE ECOSYSTEM
FOOD PYRAMID

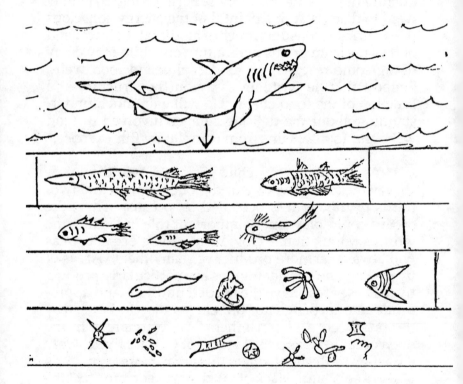

energy available from producers like phytoplankton and algae, researchers are working on methods to harvest this crop and to make it palatable for human consumption. Discuss with your child how this could be just one small step towards helping to feed the world's population.

The Carbon Cycle

Encourage your child to draw an outline of the carbon cycle. He may use the one pictured in this book, or he may prefer to use a reference book from the public library or his own personal library to create his own representation. However, if he doesn't like to draw, suggest that he use appropriate pictures from nature magazines. (See page 27 for an example of how the carbon cycle might be represented.)

Issues of *National Geographic* should provide some help in completing this project. (Many of my students have used posterboard, pictures from magazines and different colored waterbased markers to create some beautiful representations of the carbon cycle).

With the chemistry model close at hand, discuss with your child how most of the carbon in the environment is in the form of CO_2, carbon dioxide. Explain to your child that this CO_2 is available to the green plant during the second phase of photosynthesis. The CO_2 is transformed or "fixed" into carbohydrate molecules during the process. Further, organosynthetic transformations yield lipids, pigments, nucleic acids and the like to plants. Stress that the organosynthetic transformations could not occur without the photosynthesis. Thus, life as it exists would not occur if plants and algae did not have the capability to capture this energy and transform it in a way that is usable to these producers as well as to their consumers.

25

During this process, respiration occurs and some of the carbon that was fixed into organic molecules is again released back into the air. Moreover, some of the carbon is transferred to the consumer who eats the plant. Once again, more carbon is lost during the respiration and metabolism of the consumer. Finally, organic waste materials left behind from the plant and animal are converted to usable inorganic materials by the decomposing microbial flora found in the soil.

Not all of the carbon is recycled back into the atmosphere. Carbon may be locked up in dead plants and animals buried deep beneath the earth. Much later, these fossils are used for fuel by burning. Discuss with your child that by burning fossil fuels carbon is again released into the environment via CO_2.

The Nitrogen Cycle

Explain to your child that approximately 78% of the air consists of N_2, nitrogen gas. This element is also found in the earth's crust via ammonium nitrate and sodium nitrate. Like carbon, nitrogen is needed for the formation of amino acids and for other essential biochemical processes.

The plant uses nitrogen, in the form of nitrates, to build organic compounds. When the plant dies the nitrogen is returned to the soil. The chemical change of organic nitrogen to nitrate consists of three steps. First, the decomposer microorganisms change the nitrogen-organic compounds into ammonia. A special microorganism, called nitrosomonas changes the ammonia to nitrite. This microorganism is unique because it is considered to be chemoautotrophic. Have your child dissect the word "chemoautotrophic". "Chemo" refers to chemicals, "auto" refers to self and "troph" refers to nourishment. Therefore, the chemoautotrophic nitrosomonas can change one chemical into another. An-

CARBON CYCLE

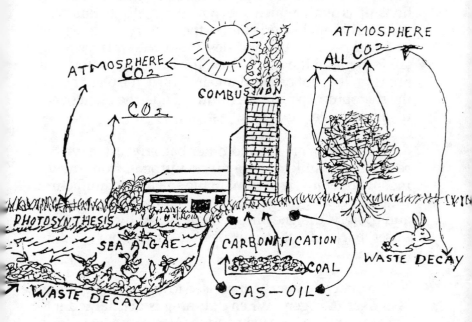

other chemoautotrophic organism, the nitrobacter, takes the nitrite and coverts it into nitrate. Now, the nitrate is available to the plant through its roots. Once again, these nitrates are used to build organic compounds.

Another way that nitrogen is fixed is by the mutualistic relationship of legumes with the Rhizobium bacteria. Explain to your child that a mutualistic relationship is one in which both parties benefit. In this case, the Rhizobium bacteria enters the roots of legumes, i.e. beans or peas. Many nodules, filled with this bacteria, are formed on the root. Thus, the bacteria has found a home on the root of the plant. In return, the plant needs the rhizobium to produce nitrate. Thus, the plant benefits from this arrangement as well.

Blue-green algae and other bacteria also have the capability to utilize some of the nitrogen from the atmosphere which is present in the soil and manufacture usable organic nitrogenous compounds. Once the algae and bacteria die, the nitrogen is recycled by the decomposer bacteria. This nitrogen is then converted to ammonia.

Your child may be surprised to learn that lightning also fixes nitrogen. When lightning is discharged into the atmosphere, nitrogen and oxygen combine to form nitric oxide. This nitric oxide combines with water H_2O in the atmosphere to produce nitric acid. The nitric acid is then deposited into the soil by the rain. This nitric acid is also capable of "fixing" with nitrates.

By studying the carbon and nitrogen cycles, your child is beginning to discover the relationship of chemistry to the environment around him. He sees that there are many intricate steps involved in breaking down and building up chemical compounds and that many types of organisms and atmospheric conditions are involved in this chemical process. Most likely, he will find the study of these cycles to be quite intriguing.

You can increase your child's understanding of the intricate balance of plant and animal life to prevailing climatic conditions by devoting part of this lesson to the study of the biomes of the world. Suggest that your child look up the meaning of the word "biome". He will discover that this word means a locale which has a distinct type of flora and fauna indigenous to it. Further suggest that your child draw a representation of the world map and color code the different biomes of the world (See page 30).

Next, encourage your child to write a report about the biomes of the world. His report should be well organized and long enough to give the reader an understanding of the characteristics of each of the biomes. He will need to devote some time to researching the types of flora and fauna found in each of the biomes. Suggest that he also give you and possibly a small audience an oral report of his findings. He may wish to use the map that he drew as a reference point throughout his written and oral report. Such an exercise combines English composition with speaking skills as well as strengthening research skills needed for further scientific study.

The Water Cycle

By now your child is discovering that "water" is one of the key ingredients to the proliferation of plant and animal life. He sees the tropical rain forest as one in which the environment is teeming with various plants and animals. Conversely, in the desert regions, he sees that the lack of water results in a decreased number of flora and fauna.

BIOMES OF THE WORLD

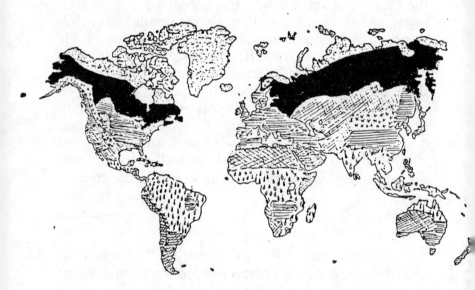

POLAR

COLD

MODERATE

DRY REGION

MTS.

TROPICAL RAIN

A chart, like the one pictured on page 32, is often useful when discussing the water cycle. Explain to your child that the water cycle is continuous; there is no beginning or end. However, for purposes of instruction, you may want to begin your discussion by explaining that water which is evaporated from the ground and ocean becomes water vapor. The water vapor forms clouds. Thus, condensation occurs. The water, from these clouds, is released back to the land and ocean by precipitation. Over 70% of this water falls back into the ocean. The rest falls on land.

Discovering the Magic Properties of Water

Maria Montessori advocated the use of "hands on" activities when presenting new concepts to students. She felt that the student could more fully appreciate the idea presented if he could somehow experience it. Thus, the following simple chemistry experiments will give your child an opportunity to make "solutions", to see the relevance of the words "solute", "solvent" and "saturated" and to appreciate the many properties of water.

For the first experiment your child will need an eight ounce glass, a teaspoon, 3/4 cup of sugar, and water. First, ask your child to fill the glass with water. Then, instruct him to place a teaspoonful of sugar into the glass. Explain that the water should be stirred until the sugar is completely dissolved. Have him continue to add and stir one teaspoonful of sugar into the glass at a time, each time checking to see what changes occur. Explain that when the glass of water begins to look cloudy, the water is considered to be "saturated" with sugar. Further explain that in this experiment the water is called the "solvent". A liquid which can dissolve substances or solids, i.e. sugar, is called a "solvent". The solid or substance is referred to as the "solute". So, in this experiment the sugar is the "solute". When a

31

THE WATER CYCLE

"solute" is dissolved in a "solvent" a "solution" is created.

To solidify the concept introduced in the first experiment your child may enjoy making another solution with a different solute. In this next experiment the "solute" will be salt rather than sugar. Ask your child to follow the instructions given in the first experiment, substituting the solute "salt" for "sugar". Ask your child to add and stir salt into the glass of water, until the water becomes saturated. Then discuss how the ocean water is able to dissolve many solutes that are continually emptied into it.

As your child has discovered throughout this lesson, water is one of the most unique materials of nature. Besides its function as a super solvent, water is also capable of breaking apart small rocks and moving these rock particles a great distance. These particles are often referred to as sediments. Sediments not only come from oceanic waters but from streams and rivers that enter the oceans as well.

Eventually, these sediments settle to the bottom of oceans or lakes where they form sedimentary rocks. Approximately 22% of all sedimentary rocks form from chemicals like carbonate, calcium, potassium, sulfate and magnesium to name a few. Also, as mentioned before, certain forms of marine life like corals and sea urchins extract calcium carbonate from the surrounding waters to make their protective shells. Once these organisms die, the shells can become part of the sediments that settle and form limestone.

Since sedimentary rocks are the most abundant of all rocks found on earth, your child might enjoy learning how to classify and identify these rocks. This "hands-on" exercise requires looking around your neighborhood for some of the specimens and visiting your local rock shop to obtain additional samples. If you are unable to obtain all of the types needed, look in Appendix D for the name and address of a rock shop which will be happy to serve you by mail.

The scientific community relies on classification to help identify and study animate and inanimate objects. For example, rocks can be classified according to hardness. By following the scale of hardness, your child will be able to easily classify rocks.

SCALE OF HARDNESS

1. TALC
2. GYPSUM
3. CALCITE
4. FLOURITE
5. APATITE
6. FELDSPAR
7. QUARTZ
8. TOPAZ
9. CORUNDUM
10. DIAMOND

Explain to your child that rocks can be classified according to hardness. For example, Talc, which can be scratched by a fingernail, is designated as being the softest. Gypsum, which can also be scratched by your fingernail rates as second on the list. Calcite, which rates third, can be scratched by a penny. Flourite, which can be scratched by a sharp instrument, like a knife, is fourth on the list of hardness. Apatite, which can also be scratched by a very sharp instrument, rates fifth on the list. Note, at this point, that apatite will also easily scratch any other rock that rates lower than itself. Feldspar rates sixth on the list, because it is harder than a sharp instrument. Thus, a scratch can usually be produced on the surface of a knife by Feldspar. Quartz, which rates seventh, can easily scratch the surface of glass. In eighth place, we find Topaz. Topaz will easily scratch the surface of Quartz. Corundum, which rates ninth on the list of hardness, will scratch Topaz as well as any other rock in the one through eight category. The Diamond, which is the hardest, will easily scratch any of the rocks in the one through nine category.

Further, rocks may be classified according to specific types. For this lesson, you will want to concentrate on presenting the sedimentary rocks classification, since relevant topics like the water cycle, coral reef formation and the previously mentioned chemistry applications relate to the formation of sedimentary rocks.

Sandstone
Sandstone is perhaps one of the most interesting rocks to study. With a sample in hand, point out the circular, rippling marks on the specimen. Explain that these markings indicate that the rock was made in a water environment. Further explain that sandstone comes in numerous colors. Brown sandstone and white sandstone are most commonly seen, but specimens of gray sandstone and white sandstone are also seen in many regions of the country. The color of the sandstone is due to the mineral composition. For example, white sandstone is composed of quartz. Brown sandstone, on the other hand, contains hermatite, which is a brown iron mineral.

Limestone
Limestone, as mentioned earlier, is formed primarily from the shells of certain marine organisms. Limestone is usually white; however, if other minerals become embedded in it, the color of this sedimentary rock may change to a gray or tan.

Conglomerate Rock

A conglomerate rock consists of a mixture of different stones. Some of these stones are quite large; others are quite minute. These stones are glued together by a base such as limestone or sandstone. Conglomerates are usually formed by fast moving streams or river beds. These stones are pushed rapidly through the streams; they then settle one on top of another, explaining the random sizes of the stones making up the conglomerates.

Shale

Shale consists of fine mud particles. The mineral composition usually includes mica and clay. This sedimentary rock is quite soft in consistency, yet, it is uniquely waterproof. Your child may be somewhat familiar with the term *oil shales*. The derivative from these oil shales is petroleum; thus, oil shales have been used by many industries worldwide.

• • •

You began this lesson by presenting the "work" of the coral. Through this odyssey your child has discovered that in order for the coral to survive and proliferate, a precious balance must be maintained.

Coral growth proliferates when certain nutrients are available and the water temperature is just right. A harmonious relationship with other aquatic members of the community also helps to insure the coral's survival.

Your child sees the role of photosynthesis as one where vital energy is fixed. He further learns how this energy is utilized by the producer organisms and subsequent consumer organisms. By analyzing the food chain, he becomes further aware of the interdependence that organisms have with one another.

Your child also begins to understand the importance of maintaining the delicate balance of the carbon
and nitrogen cycles. He sees that many steps are involved in the formation of usable organic nitrogen and
carbon compounds, and that an equally complex set of
steps are required for the decomposition of organic
substances into inorganic substances. By studying these
cycles your child also learns about the importance of
recycling.

By learning about the water cycle, your child sees
how and where water is distributed. He further discovers that water aids in erosion. It is because of this
property that chemicals are broken down and become
available to plant and animal life. The properties of
water are of particular importance to the coral because
of its dependence on these chemicals for survival.

Because Maria Montessori felt that older children
learn much through *imagination*, chemical models, maps,
simple chemistry experiments and rock classification
exercises have been used to help your child visualize the
concepts being presented. Now, your child is ready to
put his new found knowledge to practical use.

Caretakers of the Planet

The last presentations of this science lesson are
aimed at helping your child see his role as caretaker of
the environment. For the last year or so the media has
awakened the public's consciousness to the perils our
planet will face unless each one of us responds to the
mounting warning signs. Thus, it is our responsibility
as teachers and parents to present lessons that will spark
creative problem solving and motivate student partici-
pation in environmental matters.

Begin this last lesson by discussing an environmental concern close to home. Mention that during the late 1980's and early 1990's the coral reef in Key Largo, Florida has suffered extensive damage. For example, during November 1989 over 1,000 square feet of the reef was damaged when a freighter ran aground. Discuss with your child the ramifications of such an accident.

The continual disruption of the coral reef in Key Largo, Florida is unfortuately just one of many factors involved with the worldwide destruction of coral reefs. Other factors include the dumping of sewage and fertilizers into the tropical waterways.

In addition to the pollution problem, the coral reef of Key Largo, Florida is also vulnerable to recreational injury from vacationers and native small boat owners. Often, without thinking, the boat owners sink their anchors against the reef. This leads to further disruption of the marine community. However, the concerned people of Key Largo are campaigning to make all of their citizens and tourists environmentally aware. They realize that this destruction cannot continue.

Residents of the area are installing mooring buoys as a protective measure against the anchors. Moreover, they are also addressing the pollution problem. However, because pollution is a political issue the resolution may not be as immediate. Impress upon your child that action rather than passivity will make the difference.

As a consumer, your child can also make a difference. Plan to take a mini-field trip with your child to the grocery store. Select different items and invite your child to read the labels. Perhaps you have already encouraged him to look for terms like sucrose, polyunsaturated fats, monounsaturated fats, hydrogenated fats, low sodium, cholesterol free and so on. If so good!

Now, educate him about some new ingredients to look for. Ask him to pick up a carton of laundry detergent or dishwashing detergent. Have him check to see if the word "phosphates" appears on the label. If it does, explain that phosphates pollute our waterways.

Some children are highly curious and inquisitive as to what eventually happens to the household water, i.e. from bathing, dishwashing, cooking and eliminating. So be prepared to digress for a moment in your presentation. Explain that this water is carried through pipes to a water treatment plant. In some regions of the country, personnel at the water treatment plants are very accommodating, so you may want to schedule a field trip.

The field trip is not at all distasteful. Rather, it is quite educational. Children learn about the various steps involved in water treatment. Obviously, some of the areas are off limits, but children acquire enough knowledge to satisfy their curiosity about how the water is handled and routed.

Removing phosphates from the water is expensive; thus, it may not be done at the treatment plant. Thus, "phosphates" or phosphorus may be released into the waterways causing a proliferation of algal growth. As mentioned before, oxygen is depleted and marine life suffers the consequences.

The Chlorofluorocarbon Controversy

Now, ask your child to read the labels on some of the aerosol spray cans. Have him check to see if the following words appear: Chlorofluorocarbon, or derivatives like CFC-11; Trichlorofluoromethane, CFC-12; Dichlorodifluoromethane, CFC-113 ; Trichtorotrifluoroethane, CFC-114 ; and Monochloropentafluoroethane, CFC-115. If one of these terms is noted on the label, explain that chlorofluorocarbons or CFC's penetrate the ozone layer, creating holes, particularly in areas above the Arctic and Antarctic regions. Further explain that the ozone layer is a protective shield above the earth which acts as a filter. Its height is usually about 15 to 20 miles. The ozone's function is to protect all life forms from the sun's harmful high-energy radiation, also known as UV, ultraviolet radiation.

Scientists believe that they have discovered a correlation between an increased amount of ultraviolet radiation which is currently penetrating the earth's atmosphere to a higher incidence of skin cancer. Consequently, scientists have warned the public that in order to protect the ozone layer from further damage, we must drastically limit the amount of CFC products that we use.

While at the supermarket discuss the packaging of products. Explain that products packaged in aluminum or glass may be a better investment for our environment than products packaged in plastic. As you know, most plastics don't decompose, although some can be recycled. However, the process may be costly. If you must buy a product packed in plastic, make certain that it is the new bonafide biodegradable type.

Conversely, aluminum and glass can easily be recycled. Whenever possible, encourage your child to select an aluminum or glass packaged item. Later, when you get home you can discuss a home recycling program with him.

Starting a Home or School Recycling Program

You may want to obtain a copy of a free brochure entitled *"If You're Not Recycling You're Throwing It All Away"*, published by The Environmental Defense Fund. Write to the publisher at 257 Park Avenue South, New

York, New York 10010 or call (800) 225-5333. Start your recycling program by asking members of your household to place the aluminum, glass, and paper recyclables into different containers. Place all of your aluminum waste products in one container. In another container, place your waste paper, and so forth. Hopefully, your child will be an enthusiastic participant. Encourage him to initiate and maintain this program at home. Your child may want to contact your local department of sanitation and inquire as to the location of the closest recycling center. Some communities already have flexible recycling centers in place where eager volunteers will come to the home and pick up the recyclables.

Your child may also want to recruit his friends to help initiate a "keep the community clean" project. **Keep America Beautiful** will gladly help your child organize such a program. For more information write **Keep America Beautiful**, 9 West Broad Street, Stamford, Connecticut 06892.

Both teachers and parents will want to contact the National Recycling Coalition at 1101 30th Street, NW, Suite #305, Washington, D.C. 20007 for additional information about recycling. Specify whether you want to organize a recycling program at school or at home. You'll be delighted with the information that you receive.

The Greenhouse Effect

As your child has learned, the ozone protects the earth from the sun's damaging ultraviolet radiation. However, carbon dioxide CO_2 also plays an important role in stabilizing the earth's atmosphere. Excessive amounts of CO_2 spewed into the air cause too much heat to be trapped into the atmosphere. Burning fossil fuels, particularly coal, gas, and oil contributes to most of the excessive CO_2 that is released into the atmosphere.

The burning of the precious rain forests in South America also results in large quantities of CO_2 being released. Concurrently, the absence of these trees results in upsetting the natural conversion of CO_2 to O_2. While man converts O_2 to CO_2, trees and plants use the CO_2 to make O_2. For additional information on the tropical rain forest issue write to the **World Wildlife Fund**, 1250 24th Street, NW, Washington, D.C. 20037.

Because of the increase in atmospheric CO_2 scientists are worried that global warming will occur. If the earth's temperature rises too high many ecosystems will be affected. The glaciers in both hemispheres could melt and the ocean levels could concurrently rise. At present, there is some disagreement within the scientific community on just how the marine life would be affected by increased temperatures.

However, there is little disagreement as to how global warming would affect agriculture. Excessive heat discourages some crops from growing. Other crops are very sensitive to numerous factors including the amount and duration of sunshine, rainfall, and frost, to name a few. A variation in the climate could yield fewer crops.

Obviously, you want your child to be concerned, not obsessed with worry, about the environmental issues facing us today. Your child will feel that "he" has some control over the situation if he becomes an active participant. Moreover, by becoming involved, he learns more about nature and how to interact constructively with it.

One project that your child will enjoy involves organizing a tree planting project in his community. Trees help to absorb CO_2 and convert it to O_2, so the more trees we plant, the better our environment will be for our concerted effort. For information on this project contact the **American Forestry Association**, Global Releaf, P.O. Box 2000, Washington, D.C. 20013.

Your child will undoubtedly want to learn more about environmental issues. Therefore, I highly recommend reading "Save Our Planet" and "50 Simple Things You Can Do To Save the Earth". Both should be available at your local library or favorite bookstore. Your family can discuss many of the excellent ideas presented in these books and implement an environmental awareness program in your home community.

LESSONS IN HEALTH
FOR FIFTH, SIXTH AND
SEVENTH GRADERS

CHAPTER III

Children are often told that in order to maintain good health, they must eat a balanced diet. Yet, they generally fail to see the true relevance of doing so. With some creative lesson planning, you can make the study of health both fun and meaningful. By taking an in-depth look at the cell, your child will see the importance of establishing good eating habits.

Begin by this unit on health, by explaining that cells make up the basic units of all living things, both plant and animal. The primary components of the cell are the cell membrane, cytoplasm and nucleus. However, when referring to plants, the term cell wall rather than cell membrane is used.

The cell is bathed in a fluid called protoplasm. Within the nucleus the protoplasm is referred to as nucleoplasm; while protoplasm found outside the cell is commonly labeled as cytoplasm. Protoplasm, which is primarily aqueous in nature, contains crucial minerals and proteins needed to maintain cellular respiration and metabolism. The proteins are composed principally of carbon, hydrogen, oxygen and nitrogen. As illustrated on page 45, the cell is a highly organized unit, assigning each organelle with a specialized function.

CELL DIAGRAM

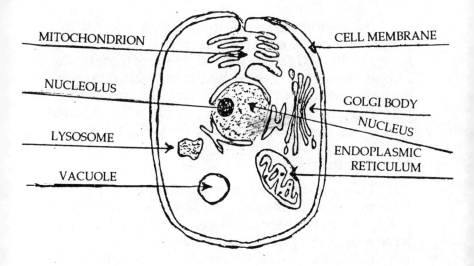

MITOCHONDRION

CELL MEMBRANE

NUCLEOLUS

GOLGI BODY

NUCLEUS

LYSOSOME

ENDOPLASMIC
RETICULUM

VACUOLE

Labels Mitochondrion
and Endoplasmic Ret.
should be reversed

Endoplasmic Reticulum

Like all of the organelles, the endoplasmic reticulum, is bathed in the cytoplasm. The endoplasmic reticulum, or ER, is perhaps one of the most fascinating organelles of the cell. It is here where protein synthesis occurs. Many of the vesicles, located on the outer region of the endoplasmic reticulum are marked with circular granules of ribonucleic acid, often abbreviated as RNA. These granules, called ribosomes, have an integral role in protein synthesis.

The endoplasmic reticulum, often referred to as the skeleton of the cell, is also responsible for the distribution of fats and carbohydrates. Many of these fats and carbohydrates are formed by the nucleolus; however, the arrangement of these nutrients for packaging is performed by the endoplasmic reticulum. The ultimate packaging, however, is done by the Golgi body.

Mitochondria

The mitochondria are often referred to as the "powerhouse" of the cell. Without the mitochondria, life as we know it would not exist. The mitochondria have special enzymes which act as catalysts in producing the energy needed for cellular respiration and metabolism. (Explain to your child that an enzyme causes a chemical reaction to occur; however, it does not become part of the reaction.)

Lysosome

Enzymes are also responsible for the digestive activities of the cell. The lysosome uses digestive enzymes to breakdown chemicals. Although, enzymes are involved in the chemical activity of both the organelles, the assigned function of lysosome containing enzymes differs immensely from the function assigned to the mitochondrial enzymes.

The Cell Membrane

The cell membrane, in which the organelles are housed, acts as a semipermeable membrane, allowing certain chemicals in while excluding others. For example, it helps to maintain a consistent ratio of potassium to sodium in the body, by allowing large concentrations of potassium to remain in the cell while keeping large concentrations of sodium out. Moreover, it attempts to keep out bacteria, viruses and other harmful agents. Obviously, some bacteria and viruses do make their way into the cell causing disease to the host. However, because of the cell membrane's protective mechanism, the myriad of disease producing agents which continually bombard the cell is kept in check.

Nucleus

The nucleus, considered to be the "hub" of the cell, is located in the nucleoplasm, which as mentioned before, is a continuation of the protoplasm. All living cells must have a nucleus to insure survival and reproduction. However, the red blood cell, known as the erythrocyte, loses its nucleus upon entering the blood stream. Its survival is limited to only about 120 days. Fortunately, a stream of erythrocytes are constantly added to the bloodstream, so the limited lifespan of an erythrocyte is not a problem.

The nucleus controls the activities of the cell; however, it is the DNA, deoxyribonucleic acid, which lays out the masterplan. Chromosomes consist primarily of DNA, and it is on these chromosomes where genes may be found.

DNA is restricted to the nucleus, while RNA may be found in both the nucleolus and mitochondria. Although, as mentioned before, RNA is a vital part of protein synthesis and transcription, it is DNA which directs the RNA to make proteins.

Cellular Functions

The cells are held together by a gelatinous fluid called intercellular material. "Inter" means between; thus, intercellular material differs in consistency according to the types of cells it binds together. For example, the intercellular material between bones is quite solid, whereas, the intercellular material between the muscle cells is more elastic.

Explain to your child that cells are the building blocks of the various tissues in the body. For example, nerve cells form nerve tissue, while muscle cells form muscle tissue. Further explain that it is the DNA which dictates what type of cell is formed.

Reproduction of Cells

As mentioned before, a cell needs a nucleus to survive. An erythrocyte loses its nucleus quite early; thus, its lifespan is short-lived. Other cells usually have a much longer lifespan, due to the presence of a nucleus. If the nucleated cell does become worn out or injured, the cell is prepared to reproduce itself.

A cell reproduces itself by dividing in two. This process is known as mitosis. There are four stages of mitosis, beginning with the prophase and ending with the telophase. The term interphase is used when referring to a cell which is not undergoing mitosis.

Look on page 49 for an illustration of the stages of mitosis. Notice the magnificent changes occurring in the nucleus of the cell. Explain to your child that it is the DNA in the nucleus which has directed the cell to reproduce.

Next, make an illustration of the process of mitosis. Use the picture on page 49 as a guide.

CELL DIVISION

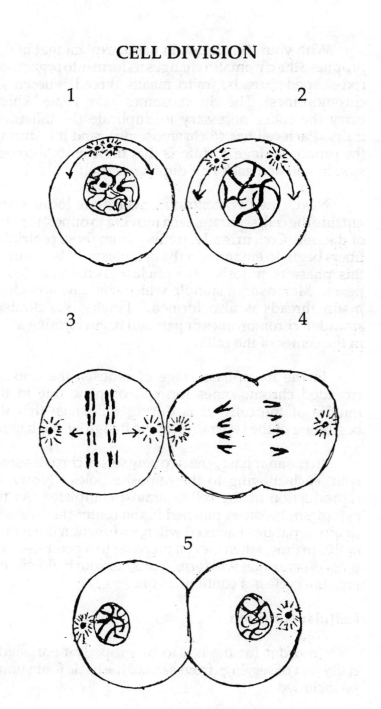

With your illustration in hand, explain that in the prophase the chromatin changes its form into organized rod-shaped threads, (mito means thread) known as chromosomes. The chromosomes have genes which carry the codes necessary to duplicate the inherited traits. Each cell has 46 chromosomes, and it is during the prophase stage of mitosis that these chromosomes split in half and each half duplicates itself.

Next, the two centrioles, which are located just outside the cell, separate, each moving to opposite poles of the cell. Concurrently, trailing from these centrioles fibers begin to emanate in the cytoplasm. Also, during this phase of mitosis, the nuclear membrane disappears. Moreover, a spindle which contains non-chromatin threads is also formed. Finally, the double-stranded chromosomes depart and begin forming a line in the center of the cell.

In the metaphase stage of mitosis, the double-stranded chromosomes form a complete line in the middle of the cell. It is during this stage that the beginning of the separation of the daughter cell begins.

In the anaphase, the two new sets of chromosomes split, each moving to the opposite poles. Now, the reproduction of the cell is almost complete. As the cytoplasm becomes pinched in the center the two cells finally separate. Each cell will now function independently. In time, when the cell prepares to reproduce, new pairs of centrioles will form. Thus, as your child discovers, the cycle is a continuous one.

Cellular Nutrition

In order for the cell to be properly nourished a daily diet of servings from each of the basic four should be included.

Protein, a nutrient needed by all cells, must first be broken down into amino acids. Explain that these amino acids are small enough to enter the cell membrane. The cell takes the amino acids and assembles them into the different proteins that are needed.

If the diet is deficient in protein, the endoplasmic reticulum loses its ability to assemble the proteins for the cells. Without this needed protein cells cannot grow properly. A protein deficient diet is particularly deleterious to the young child, causing mental and physical developmental delay. If the protein is restricted for an extended period of time, permanent damage ensues. Unfortunately, the effects of such a diet are seen in the children living in some of the third world countries.

Carbohydrates and Fats

Carbohydrates and fats are also used to help maintain cellular metabolism. Like proteins, carbohydrates and fats must be broken down. Carbohydrates are broken down into the simple sugar, glucose. Glucose and fats then combine to form triglycerides. The triglycerides enter the cell membrane and migrate to the mitochondria. Once in the mitochondria, the triglycerides combine with oxygen, thereby releasing energy.

As a parent or teacher you may want to incorporate a detailed outline specifying certain principles that you wish to present during the second part of this unit. If you feel that you are a little rusty in the area of nutrition, borrow a few books on the subject from your local library and bone-up on food sources, nutritional requirements and deficiency diseases resulting from an unbalanced diet and/or absorption problems. Once you feel that you are well prepared, consider writing your objectives on a sheet of paper to insure a smooth presentation. You may find the following example helpful for the presentation of vitamins and minerals.

Comprehension Skills
1. Child should be able to distinguish between vitamins and minerals.
2. Child should be able to differentiate between fat-soluble and water soluble vitamins.
3. Child should be able to define deficiency diseases caused by lack of
   a. vitamins
   b. minerals
4. Child should be able to classify and define signs and symptoms of vitamin and mineral deficiency diseases.
5. Child should be able to catalog foods according to vitamin and mineral content.

Appreciation of Concepts
1. Child sees that lack of sufficient vitamins and minerals interferes with good health.
2. Child appreciates how a diet containing appropriate vitamins and minerals promotes good health.
3. Child develops an appreciation of the role he plays in combating deficiency diseases by including appropriate food selections in his diet.

Developing Appropriate Health Skills
1. Child develops the research skills needed to locate information about:
   a. causes of vitamin & mineral deficiency diseases
   b. the effects of the diseases
   c. symptomatology of deficiency diseases
2. Child develops analytical skills needed to evaluate health habits in relationship to eating.

The primary emphasis in teaching good nutritional habits to students from K-12 has focused upon the basic foundation of how to creatively incorporate the correct balance of carbohydrates, proteins and fats into the diet. Although a student needs to consider the basics of good nutrition when choosing foods to include in his diet, I feel that the "basics" of nutrition should be augmented by a thorough discussion on the paramount role of essential vitamins and minerals.

The following lesson plan may be incorporated into the classroom setting or traditional home environment.

CONCEPT TO BE TAUGHT: Minerals and vitamins play a vital role in protecting the human body from disease.

METHOD: Bulletin Board – Presenter should construct a colorful collage and place it on posterboard or bulletin board. Any item pertaining to vitamins and minerals, i.e. from children's magazines, health magazines, labels from vitamin bottles, and the like should be creatively assembled so that the collage is eye catching. Next, using construction paper, cut oblong shapes to resemble vitamin pills. Brainstorm about interesting facts about vitamins and minerals that you know your child or students would find intriguing. Make questions out of these facts and encourage your students or child to do some research to discover the answers. The questions should be thought provoking so that your discussions will be stimulating. Next, place the questions on the oblong shapes.

Name the Vitamin

Vitamin A, B complex, C, D, E, K. Emphasize that there is one principal difference between the collective vitamin group. Vitamins A, D, E, K are found in fatty foods such as cream and butter. They are stable, i.e. not dissolved by water. Conversely, Vitamins B and C are water soluble and can be easily destroyed during the cooking process or from exposure to air for prolonged periods of time.

Examining the Vitamins Individually
Have the student list foods which are high in the given vitamin.

Vitamin A
1. Involved in maintaining healthy
   a. skin
   b. membranes which line interior portions of the body, i.e. mouth, stomach
2. Assists in the formation and maintenance of healthy teeth
3. Essential for health of gums and growth of bones
4. Principal role in night vision

What happens if we have an insufficient amount of Vitamin A in our diet?
1. Increased susceptibility to colds and flu
2. Acne
3. Inability to see well at night

Foods that are rich in Vitamin A are **carrots, peas, apples, plums, squash, eggs, butter, pumpkin and cheddar cheese.**

Vitamin D
1. Essential for proper development of bones and teeth

What happens if we have an insufficient amount of vitamin D in our diet?
1. Rickets
2. Poor growth
3. Fatigue

Foods that are rich in Vitamin D are **milk, tuna, salmon; insufficient exposure to sunlight will also result in susceptibility to aforementioned conditions**

Vitamin E
1. Serves to protect all the other fatty vitamins
2. Assists in the production of new blood vessels in damaged regions of the body.

What happens if we have an insufficient amount of Vitamin E in our diet?
1. Interferes with growth

Best food sources of Vitamin E are **cereals, wheat germ products, green vegetables**

Vitamin K
1. Assists in the clotting of blood

What happens if we have an insufficient amount of Vitamin K in our diet?
1. Blood doesn't clot properly
2. Internal bleeding may occur

Best food sources of Vitamin K are **soybeans, alfalfa, green leafy vegetables**

Vitamin C
1. Assists in healing
2. Supports our skin, cartilage, tendons, and bones
3. Protects us from infections (bacterial & viral infections)

What happens if we have an insufficient amount of Vitamin C in our diet?
1. Painful gums
2. Loss of hair
3. Tiredness
4. Bleeding gums
5. Scurvy

Best food sources of Vitamin C are **oranges, limes, lettuce, tomato, lemon, grapefruit**

Vitamin B Complex (Concentrate on presenting Thiamin, Riboflavin, Niacin, B12)
1. Stabilizes the appetite
2. Needed to maintain a normally functioning nervous system

What happens if we have an insufficient amount of Vitamin B Complex in our diet?
1. "Fire engine" red tongue
2. Canker sores in the mouth
3. Loss of appetite
4. Dizziness
5. Nervousness

Best sources of Vitamin B Complex are **milk, rice, wheat containing products, cereals, breads.**

Although Thiamin, Riboflavin, Niacin and B12 are regarded singularly as well as collectively, I have grouped them together for ease of discussion.

Learning Exercise

Students are to list the vitamins and minerals contained in the everyday foods that they consume. EXAMPLES: Milk, cereals, bread, fruit juices, junk food, and so on.

METHOD: Each student is encouraged to keep a daily diary of all foods consumed. At the end of the day, the student will list all foods eaten, according to vitamin and mineral content. For example, milk products would be listed under the headings of calcium and vitamin D.

Students should be encouraged to read labels of all canned foods, frozen dinners, etc. to determine the total vitamin and mineral content of all natural as well as prepared food items consumed on a daily basis.

Hopefully, students will be more familiar with the "true content" of foods by reading the various labels carefully.

PART II

Selected Mineral Analysis

Focus on this next section will be on analyzing each of the minerals.

Calcium
1. Assists in clotting of blood
2. Required for proper nerve and muscle functioning

What happens if we have an insufficient amount of calcium in our diet?
1. Poor formation of bones and teeth
2. Leg cramps
3. Nervousness

Encourage students to glance at the lists they compiled of food consumed daily.

For example: Prompt by asking leading questions. Which foods contain calcium? Student will list foods high in calcium, i.e. milk, yogurt, cheese, etc.

Phosphorus
1. Formation of strong bones and teeth

What happens if we have an insufficient amount of phosphorus in our diet?
1. Poor bone and tooth formation

Prompt…Which foods contain phosphorus?

TYPICAL RESPONSE: Milk, meat, and so forth. Once again, students use their personal lists to determine if they are consuming phosphorus rich foods.

Potassium
1. Assists in nerve and muscle function.
2. Regulator in our body. (Review function potassium has in cellular metabolism.)

Sodium
1. Works with potassium.
2. If we have an inadequate amount of sodium in our diet (which is unusual) we may become dehydrated. However, too much sodium (salt) can cause high blood pressure and kidney disease. Therefore, we should avoid consuming salted foods.

<u>Magnesium</u>
1. Necessary for contraction of muscles

What may a deficiency result in?
1. Impaired nerve and muscle function

Best source is **milk**.

<u>Iron</u>
1. Helps blood to carry oxygen
2. Review erythrocytes (RBC's) with your students.

What may a deficiency result in?
1. Anemia (inability of blood to carry oxygen)
2. Lack of appetite

Best sources are **Boston baked beans and fish**.

<u>Iodine</u>
1. Helps thyroid and body's metabolism

What happens if we don't consume enough iodine?
1. Goiter
2. Slow mental reactions
3. Dry, brittle hair
Best sources are **iodized salt and fish**.

<u>Flourine</u>
1. Helps strengthen bones and teeth

What happens if we don't consume enough flourine?
1. Poor tooth development

What are some sources for flourine? **Water** (in some areas) and **toothpaste** (Point out that too much flourine may also be harmful.)

Zinc
1.   Helpful in healing of wounds, burns, etc.

What happens if we don't consume enough zinc?
1.   Tiredness
2.   Slow healing

What are some sources? **Milk**

The above lesson plan is just a skeleton of what you will want to present to your child or group of students. Your role is to present the basics of vitamins and minerals, while encouraging the child to do outside research, i.e. at the library on the types of food sources, deficiency diseases and health applications of each of these nutrients.

You have laid the groundwork by stimulating your child's imagination of how the cell depends on nutrients to maintain homeostasis within the organism. He sees that the cell cannot function properly without these nutrients. Cells are the fundamental units of tissue. Tissue forms organs and organs are part of the major body systems.

By analyzing his own diet, he sees his responsibility in selecting the appropriate foods to maintain good health. He sees that the consequences of eating an unbalanced diet will result in disease; thus, he chooses to make wise food selections a part of his daily lifestyle.

LESSONS IN SOCIAL STUDIES
FOR FIFTH, SIXTH AND
SEVENTH GRADERS
CHAPTER IV

In order for a child to fully appreciate the significance of studying geography on a worldwide scale, he needs to first understand how geography can be applied a little closer to home. Terms like northeast, southwest, west and south will become more meaningful if he uses them to describe the location of his house to a nearby park, school, friend's house and the like. Therefore, for this first exercise you will want to draw a map of the town center of your community, illustrating the locations of significant points of interest. For example, you may want to include buildings like the post office, police station, grocery store, church or synagogue, schools, friends' houses, as well as your neighborhood park.

Use the illustration on page 62 to reinforce directional skills. Copy the illustration onto a 22" x 28" sheet of posterboard. Remember to include a drawing of the compass so that your child can refer to it during this next learning activity. Place a toy car in the intersection of Main Street and Lee Avenue. Place another car in the intersection of Rose Avenue and Main Street. Next, using index cards, write points of interest, one per card. For example, on one card you will write Sunnyvale High School. On another card write Elm Park and so on until you have included all points of interest. Then, shuffle the cards and place them face down in a pile.

Explain to your child that the two of you will be travelling to various places in town and that the object of this exercise is to be able to give clear, concise directions on how to get from one destination to another.

NEIGHBORHOOD DIRECTION GAME

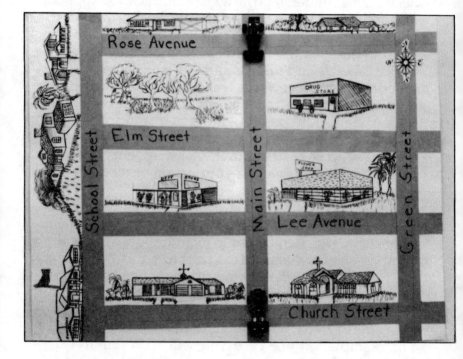

Select a card from the pile and read aloud the point of interest mentioned. For example, if you selected a card with Sunnyvale High School written on it, you will explain to your child that you will have to travel west one block until you get to the intersection of Lee Avenue and School Street. Then, you will proceed to travel south on School Street to your destination, Sunnyvale High School. As you explain, move your car along the designated path. Once you arrive at your destination, leave the car there.

Now, it is your child's turn to select a card from the pile. Let's suppose that he has selected a card with flower shop written on it. He will then proceed to move his vehicle along the path to the flower shop while orally explaining the directions of his destination. For example, he will describe that he will be travelling south on Main Street until he arrives at the flower shop. He will then leave his car at the flower shop.

Once again it becomes your turn to select a card. Let's suppose that your card has drug store written on it. Explain to your child that you could travel north on School Street until you get to the intersection of School Street and Elm Street. Then, you would travel east on Elm until you arrive at the drug store. Alternatively, you could travel north on School Street until you get to the intersection of School Street and Lee Avenue. Explain that you would travel east on Lee Avenue and north on Main Street until you arrive at your destination.

Later, you can discuss the significance of using terms like southwest, northeast and the like. You can either use the illustration on page 62 or the representation of your town center. If you decide to use the illustration in this book, you can enlarge upon the previously mentioned exercise by asking your child to tell you the relationship of his car to the destination mentioned on the card selected. For example, if your child selects a card with Elm Park written on it and his car is parked by the church on Church Street he would tell you that Elm Park is located northwest from Church Street. You, in turn, would then select a card; however, this time encourage your child to tell you which direction your car is located from the point of interest mentioned on the index card.

Discovering the Continents

Now that your child is familiar with the geography of his immediate community, you will want to spend some time discussing the locations of neighboring communities and counties in your state. Your child will undoubtedly learn the names and locations of counties in his state that were previously unfamiliar to him. Some children become quite fascinated with learning more about the geography of their state. You can foster this interest by encouraging your child to borrow some books on the state at your local library.

Naturally, your child will benefit immensely from a discussion with you about the geography and history of your state. Therefore, borrow a few books about the state in advance of your presentation, so that you will be prepared to discuss the topic in-depth. As previously mentioned, children in this age group thrive on detailed, thought provoking lessons. Hence, prepare to give thorough answers so that you will satisfy your child's inquisitive mind.

A map of the United States will also seem more relevant when you encourage your child to describe the geographical positions of one state in relation to another. Encourage your child to use the terms he has previously used to describe which states are located in the north, which are located in the midwest and so forth.

For example, your child should be able to tell you with ease which states or countries are located east, west, north, and south of Montana.

Naturally, you will also want to discuss the countries which share the North American continent with the United States. You may want to obtain a map which illustrates the entire North American continent as well as a map of the United States.

Now, focus your child's attention on examining the world as an interlocking unit. With a map which illustrates the four hemispheres or a world globe close at hand, point out the position of the western hemisphere. Explain that the continents of North America and South America are located here. Further explain that Antarctica is located on both the western and eastern hemispheres, because of its circumference around the area of the South Pole.

Other points of interest you will want to mention include the isthmus of Panama. Explain that an isthmus links two bodies of land together. In this instance, Panama joins the continents of North and South America. Ask your child to name some of the other countries in this Central American region. He has probably heard references to Nicaragua or El Salvador through the media, but he may have not known the geographical locations of many of these Central American countries until now.

The archipelago, located between North America and South America is another fascinating point of interest. Explain to your child that this archipelago represents the body of islands, collectively referred to as the West Indies. It serves as a dividing line between the Atlantic Ocean and the Caribbean Sea.

Now, direct your child's attention on the eastern hemisphere for a moment. Ask him to name which continents are located here. He should mention Africa, Asia, Australia, Antarctica, and Europe. Africa will be mentioned in-depth later in this unit, so begin this lesson on the study of the eastern hemisphere by centering your child's attention on analyzing the Asiatic continent.

Asia is a dynamic continent, composed of people with divergent political, religious and cultural orientations. As your child will notice, the largest countries in this continent are China, India, Saudi Arabia and the Soviet Union. Emphasize during your presentation that the Ural Mountains of the Soviet Union separate the continents of Asia and Europe. Thus, part of the Soviet Union is in Europe as well.

Between the continents of Asia and Australia lies another archipelago. The Archipelago of Malay consists of many islands which separates the Pacific Ocean from the Indian Ocean. New Guinea and the Philippines are just two of many islands which are a part of this archipelago.

To the west of the Ural mountains lies the region of the Soviet Union. You will want to devote some of your discussion time to covering the northern region of this continent. Be sure to spend some of your presentation time discussing the region of the Scandinavian countries in addition to the time devoted to the continuing changes which are occurring in Germany, Poland, Romania and the like. You will also want to touch on other countries of Europe, including the islands of Great Britain and Ireland.

Now, reinforce the skills learned during the first part of your social science presentation by asking your child to tell you the directions of Spain to France. Next, ask him to tell you the direction of Finland to Italy. If he seems to be enjoying this exercise, continue by asking him to describe the geographical direction of various European countries to Asiatic countries.

Now, direct your child's attention to the continent of Africa. Ask your child to locate Egypt. Children between the ages of 10 and 12 are usually intrigued by the ancient civilization of Egypt. In a subsequent chapter in this book, a detailed lesson plan on the Egyptian and Maya civilizations is outlined. Therefore, to spark some interest ask your child to locate the Nile River and the Nile Delta. Using a pencil, have him trace the flow of the Nile River northward to the Mediterranean Sea.

World Geography

Learning facts about countries can be very tedious. Realizing this, Maria Montessori designed learning activities for the preschooler and younger elementary student which would stimulate their interest in the study of geography. During these exercises the teacher made the presentation, but it was the child who ultimately made the discoveries without the interference from the teacher.

Maria Montessori's insight into the needs of the older elementary student made her aware that the learning relationship between the presenter and child would change. The presenter would need to become a more active participant in the learning activities. Therefore, as the two of you embark upon this next learning exercise guide your child through the fascinating world of geography. Remember to give your child the room to make his own discoveries, as you did when he was younger; however, now you must be intuitive enough to sense when he needs some additional guidance. You may find that your child challenges you at times, and this is natural. He seeks to find detailed answers to satisfy his never ending thirst for knowledge about the universe, and with your help this quest for understanding will be one of the most enjoyable, memorable periods in his life.

World Geography Bingo

The basic supplies needed for World Geography Bingo are identical to those mentioned in **Modern Montessori at Home** for the Phonogram Bingo Game. The amount of cards that you will need for World Geography Bingo will depend upon how many continents you wish to include in your game. Initially, I suggest presenting the countries of one continent at a time. Thus, for the first game 15 game cards will suffice. The cards should measure about 9" x 12". Use either a heavy weight construction paper or lightweight posterboard. I prefer to use the light beige colored posterboard, so that the highlighted countries can be easily visualized.

Your neighborhood stationery store or art supply store should be able to supply you with a nice selection of these items. Purchase a few extra sheets of construction paper or lightweight posterboard so that you can make plenty of markers. These markers should be the diameter of a quarter. Select any color that you like. A darker contrasting color is best. You will need six markers per game card. Initially, you and your child will play this game, so a total of twelve markers will be needed.

You may select **any continent** that you wish; however, for the purpose of this presentation, let's assume that you wish to initially present the continent of Africa. Using a sheet of white typing paper, draw a representation of the continent of Africa. Draw all of the geographical borders, but don't include the names of the countries. Look at the example on page 71. Notice that Madagascar, Seychelles, Mauritius, the Comoros Islands and Cape Verde have been included.

Next, take one of the 9" x 12" game cards and draw a line horizontally, dividing the area of the card in half. Next, draw two vertical lines so that the card is divided into six equal squares. With the game card and your representation of Africa in hand, visit your local print shop and have your representation reduced in size so that it will easily fit into one of the six squares on the game card. Then, have 90 of these reduced representations copied. Remember, that you have 15 game cards and since there are six square per card, you will need 90 representations.

Once you arrive home, you will want to enlist your child's help with the construction of this game. Ask him to glue one representation per square. Once he has finished gluing the representations onto the game cards, ask him to locate a dark crayon or marker. Then, instruct him to darken a different country on each representation. Refer to page 71 for an example of how the finished game card might look. Notice that in the first square the country of South Africa has been darkened. In the second square the country of Egypt has been darkened, while in the third square, Kenya has been darkened. In the lower left half of the card, or fourth square, Nigeria has been darkened, in the fifth square, Chad is darkened while in the lower right half the sixth square Namibia is darkened.

You and your child can continue making the remaining 14 games cards, highlighting selected countries of this continent. Discuss the locations, i.e. northwest, southeast of the various countries as well as the political, beliefs, religions, and languages spoken by the people in the various regions. Use the master copy in this book to label each of the countries in the African continent. To save time, you will probably want to use the pattern you drew on the sheet of typing paper. During the game, you will refer to this master copy to determine if your child has correctly named the country highlighted.

By constructing the game cards your child has become familiar with many of the locations of the African countries. However, now he needs to know more about the religious, political and cultural differences which make each country unique. Encourage him to borrow several books about Africa from the local library. It is best to borrow a book which was published during the late 1980's or early 1990's so that the data will be accurate. You, too, will want to borrow books on Africa so that you can review some of the data about the various countries.

Using some sheets of scratch paper, jot down pertinent information about each of the countries. You may want to include facts like population, languages spoken, religious beliefs and so on. See pages 75-82 for a sampling of facts you may wish to include. You and your child will undoubtedly want to include other categories besides those listed on pages 75 through 82. **The Young Discovery Library** has recently published a series of books designed to enlighten children of all ages about the various topics of interest, i.e. music, animals, countries and so on. Your child may want to use some of the facts found in these books for his World Geography Game. For more information about **The Young Discovery Library** see Appendix B.

Once you have compiled the information you wish to include for each of the countries, transfer the data onto index cards. You will use one index card per country represented. For example, write or type all of the data about Ghana on an index card. Next, place the number assigned to it. This number will match the number on the master sheet, so that if during the game

SAMPLE CARD FROM
WORLD GEOGRAPHY GAME

SOUTH AFRICA

EGYPT

KENYA

NIGERIA

CHAD

NAMIBIA

your child has difficulty remembering the name of the country, he can refer to the master sheet to discover its name.

You will want to enlist your child's help in transferring this information, so that he will continue to absorb knowledge about the various countries. Then, when he plays the actual game, his knowledge will be reinforced.

Once you and he have completed transferring the data onto the index cards, put the exercise aside. Montessori felt that in order for a child to truly benefit from a learning activity, his "will" must be involved. Thus, plan to actually play the World Geography Bingo Game during a subsequent learning session when the two of you feel refreshed. Then your child can assess just how much knowledge he actually gained through completing the necessary research to gather the data.

Shuffle the 15 game cards, then ask your child to select one, while you select another. Place the master sheet, which illustrates all of the countries of Africa, face down in between the two of you. Next, shuffle the index cards and place them in a single pile. Ask your child to remove the top card from the pile. Ask him to read the information, i.e. trivia, mentioned on the card about this country. After you and your child guess as to what the identity of the country might be, turn the master sheet face up to see which of you made the correct identification. Now, you and your child can examine your game cards to determine if the highlighted country is pictured. If it is not pictured on either game card, then proceed on with the game. However, if it is pictured on either card, then a marker will be placed on the square, where the highlighted country is illustrated. (In either case, be sure to place the master sheet face down before you proceed.)

Now, it is your turn to select an index card from the pile. You will follow the above example, reading the trivia mentioned on the card and surmising from the information given what the identity of the country might be. Encourage your child to guess the identity as well. Then, once again turn the master sheet face up to see if either of you gave the correct answer. Look on the game cards to see if this country is highlighted in any of the six squares. If it is, a marker will be placed over the square illustrating this African country.

The two of you will continue playing until one of you has a card with three markers across on the top row, i.e. top three squares, or three markers across on the bottom row. As in all other types of bingo, three in a row constitutes a winning card.

MASTER SHEET NUMBER CODE FOR AFRICA

1. Algeria
2. Angola
3. Benin
4. Botswana
4. Burkina
6. Burundi
7. Cameroon
8. Cape Verde
9. Central African Rep.
10. Chad
11. Comoros Islands
12. Congo
13. Djibouti
14. Egypt
15. Equatorial Guinea
16. Ethiopia
17. Gabon
18. Ghana
19. Guinea
20. Guinea-Bissau
21. Ivory Coast
22. Kenya
23. Lesotho
24. Liberia
25. Libya
26. Madagascar
27. Malawi
28. Mali
29. Mauritania
30. Mauritius
31. Morocco
32. Mozambique
33. Namibia
34. Niger
35. Nigeria
36. Republic of South Africa

37. Rwanda
38. Saotome and Principe
39. Senegal
40. Seychelles
41. Sierra Leone
42. Somalia
43. Sudan
44. Swaziland
45. Tanzania
46. The Gambia
47. Togo
48. Tunisia
49. Uganda
50. Zaire
51. Zambia
52. Zimbabwe

FACTS ABOUT THE
COUNTRIES OF AFRICA FOR
WORLD GEOGRAPHY BINGO GAME

Algeria
Language Spoken	Arabic
Religion	Islam
Bordering Countries	Morocco, Tunisia, Mali

Angola
Language Spoken	Mostly English
Religion	Mostly Christian
Bordering Countries	Zaire, Zambia, Namibia

Benin
Language Spoken	Mostly French
Religion	Catholic, Islam
Bordering Countries	Togo, Nigeria

Botswana
Language Spoken	Mostly English
Religion	Christian Minority
Bordering Countries	Zimbabwe, Namibia, Rep. of So. Africa

Burkina
Language Spoken	Mostly French
Religion	Animist, Moslem
Bordering Countries	Ghana, Mali, Ivory Coast

Burundi
Language Spoken	Kirundi, French
Religion	Catholic
Bordering Countries	Rwanda, Tanzania

Cameroon
Language Spoken	French, Sudanic, English
Religion	Catholic, Moslem, Protestant
Bordering Countries	Nigeria, Chad, Eq. Guinea, Congo

Cape Verde
Language Spoken	Crioulo, Portuguese
Religion	Catholic
Bordering Countries	Senegal, The Gambia

Central Africa Republic
Language Spoken	Mostly French
Religion	Catholic, Animist, Protestant
Bordering Countries	Chad, Cameroon

Chad
Language Spoken	French, Arabic
Religion	Mostly Moslem, Some Christianity
Bordering Countries	Niger, Sudan, Libya

Comoros Islands
Language Spoken	French, Arabic
Religion	Islam
Bordering Countries	Tanzania, Malawi

Congo
Language Spoken	Mostly French
Religion	Catholic, Protestant, Anismist
Bordering Countries	Gabon, Zaire

Djibouti
Language Spoken	Arabic, French
Religion	Islam
Bordering Countries	Ethiopia, Somalia

Egypt
Language Spoken   Arabic
Religion   Sunni Moslems, Islam
Bordering Countries   Libya, Sudan

Equatorial Guinea
Language Spoken   English, Spanish
Religion   Catholic
Bordering Countries   Gabon, Cameroon

Ethiopia
Language Spoken   Arabic, English, Semitic
Religion   Moslem, Orthodox Christian
Bordering Countries   Somalia, Kenya

Gabon
Language Spoken   French
Religion   Protestant, Catholic, Animist
Bordering Countries   Cameroon, Congo, Eq. Guinea

Ghana
Language Spoken   Mostly English
Religion   Mostly Moslem or Christian
Bordering Countries   Ivory Coast, Togo

Guinea
Language Spoken   Mostly French
Religion   Mostly Moslem
Bordering Countries   Sierra Leone, Mali

Guinea-Bissau
Language Spoken   Criolo, Portuguese
Religion   Mostly Moslem
Bordering Countries   The Gambia, Guinea

Ivory Coast
Language Spoken   Mostly French
Religion   Christian, Moslem
Bordering Countries   Ghana, Liberia

Kenya

Language Spoken	English, Swahili
Religion	Protestant, Catholic, Moslem
Bordering Countries	Somalia, Ethiopia, Uganda

Lesotho

Language Spoken	English, Sesotho
Religion	Protestant, Catholic
Bordering Countries	Swaziland, Rep. of South Africa

Liberia

Language Spoken	English
Religion	Mostly Christian and Moslem
Bordering Countries	Ivory Coast, Guinea

Libya

Language Spoken	Arabic
Religion	Moslem
Bordering Countries	Egypt, Tunisia, Niger

Madasgascar

Language Spoken	Mostly French
Religion	Christian, Moslem
Bordering Countries	Mozambique, Comoros Islands

Malawi

Language Spoken	Mostly English, Some Chichewa
Religion	Moslem, Christians, Animist
Bordering Countries	Zambia, Tanzania

Mali

Language Spoken	Bambara, French
Religion	Animist, Moslem, Christianity
Bordering Countries	Niger, Algeria

Mauritania
Language Spoken	French, Arabic
Religion	Moslem
Bordering Countries	Mali, Senegal

Mauritius
Language Spoken	English, French
Religion	Moslem, Hindu, Catholic
Bordering Countries	Madagascar

Morocco
Language Spoken	Berber, Arabic
Religion	Moslem
Bordering Countries	Algeria, Mauritania

Mozambique
Language Spoken	Mainly Portuguese
Religion	Moslem, Catholic, Animist
Bordering Countries	Malawi, Zimbabwe

Namibia
Language Spoken	English, German, Afrikaans
Religion	Protestant
Bordering Countries	Botswana, Angola

Niger
Language Spoken	French, Djerrma
Religion	Moslem, Animist
Bordering Countries	Burkina, Chad

Nigeria
Language Spoken	English, Yoruba
Religion	Christian, Moslem
Bordering Countries	Cameroon, Niger

Republic of South Africa
Language Spoken	English, Afrikaans
Religion	Catholic, Protestant
Bordering Countries	Botswana, Swaziland

Rwanda
Language Spoken	Swahili, French
Religion	Catholic, Animist
Bordering Countries	Burundi, Uganda

Saotome and Principe
Language Spoken	Portuguese
Religion	Catholic
Bordering Countries	Gabon, Eq. Guinea

Senegal
Language Spoken	Mainly French
Religion	Christian, Moslem, Animist
Bordering Countries	The Gambia, Mauritania

Seychelles
Language Spoken	French, Creole, English
Religion	Catholic, Protestant
Bordering Countries	Madagascar, Comoros Islands

Sierra Leone
Language Spoken	Mostly English
Religion	Moslem, Animist
Bordering Countries	Guinea, Liberia

Somalia
Language Spoken	Somali
Religion	Moslem
Bordering Countries	Ethiopia, Kenya

Sudan
Language Spoken	Mostly Arabic
Religion	Christian, Moslem, Animist
Bordering Countries	Egypt, Chad, Ethiopia

Swaziland
Language Spoken	English, Swazi
Religion	Catholic, Protestant
Bordering Countries	Lesotho, Mozambique

Tanzania
Language Spoken	English, Swahili
Religion	Moslem, Christian
Bordering Countries	Kenya, Malawi

The Gamia
Language Spoken	English, Wolof, Mandrinka
Religion	Christian, Animist, Moslem
Bordering Countries	Senegal, Guinea-Bissau

Togo
Language Spoken	Mostly French
Religion	Christian, Animist, Moslem
Bordering Countries	Benin, Ghana

Tunisia
Language Spoken	Arabic
Religion	Moslem
Bordering Countries	Algeria, Libya

Uganda
Language Spoken	English, Swahili
Religion	Protestant, Catholic, Moslem
Bordering Countries	Kenya, Rwanda

Zaire
Language Spoken	Mostly French
Religion	Protestant, Catholic, Animist
Bordering Countries	Congo, Angola

Zambia
Language Spoken	English, Bantu
Religion	Christian, Animist
Bordering Countries	Malawi, Zimbabwe

Zimbabwe

Language Spoken	English, Bantu
Religion	Christian, Animist
Bordering Countries	Botswana, Zambia

History Presentations

Now, when you present history lessons to your child, he will have the basic geography knowledge needed to fully comprehend the significance of the material introduced. Be sure to allow enough time during each history learning session for discussion about the geography of the countries mentioned during your presentation. A world globe or updated world map is an essential learning aid which should always be near at hand during your presentations.

I enjoy presenting history by concentrating on events which transpired during a given decade. I then compare societal concerns during that particular decade with current issues. A reading list, with books appropriate for the child's age and reading ability, is an important adjunct to your presentations. You may want to enlist the children's librarian to help you compile such a list. She will be knowledgeable about the most popular books on history; moreover, she will be able to steer you to books that would be particularly suitable for your child's age and reading level. Once you have compiled your list, encourage your child to select books to borrow from it. This supplemental reading will allow your child to examine details about historical events in greater depth. Then, during subsequent learning sessions, you can focus on subject matter that your child particularly enjoyed learning about. You can then suggest that he do additional research about that topic and write a report about it. If your child is artistic, suggest that he also draw a representation of the event or person. If he enjoys music and plays an instrument well, encourage him to study the music of that particular era. Suggest that he learn to play a song that was popular during that historical period.

In order for your child to fully appreciate the significance of the decade presented, you will have to do some in-depth research about the major events and personalities which made the decade memorable.

The 1960's: An Iconoclastic Struggle

The following account is meant to illustrate how you can capsulize the major events and people of a given decade and present them to your child in a systematic manner. Many of today's mothers will have some recollection of the 1960's. It was a very turbulent time in our history. However, mothers who were not born and raised in the United States as well as mothers born after the mid 1960's will find the account helpful in the preparation of the lesson.

Each decade in American history represents a chapter added to the volume of our ever changing society. The 1960's exemplified the dawn of a multi-revolutionary condition where neonatal ideologies were manifested into a sometimes nebulous state. The myriad of issues that were dissected and analyzed included religion, the women's movement, civil rights and poverty.

During much of the 1960's, some of the Catholics became divided on church doctrine. The Protestant factions were also under attack by conservatives and liberals alike. Criticism was directed at the Protestants for their channeling of monies into philanthropic secular activities. Some of the fundamentalists reasoned that this was an inappropriate use for church funds.

The fundamentalists simply stressed the fundamentals of religion. These ministers were often criticized by the liberal youth as preaching a "fire and brimstone" sermon. This was a turn off to many rebellious youth.

Conversely, some of the Christian churches with the exception of the LDS and Seventh Day Adventists, tried desperately to pander to the rebellious youths' new found ideologies. Jesus' image was revamped so that he would appear more 'hip'. Thus, some ministers seized upon the opportunity to utilize the meaning of the rock musical "Jesus Christ Superstar" into their sermons. This pandering to a **fraction** of the youth had a multiple effect on both young and old alike. The older adults despised this attempt to cater to the youth, while the more liberal faction applauded the ministerial attempt to integrate yet another perspective of Christ's life into the Sunday sermon.

There, of course, were many families whose faith was strengthened and deepened during these turbulent times. Their beliefs were solid and events that were transpiring around them could not change the strong Christian or Jewish beliefs in which their lives centered around. For these people, the hysteria around them about religious issues seemed ridiculous.

In addition to the traditional religion models, the emergence of various cults also arose. These cults offered yet another alternative for the youth of that decade to follow.

Zen-Krishna, the Church of Scientology, Taoism and Buddhism were also explored by many. These movements seemed to hold special significance to various factions. Some historians contend that the youth of the 1960's were experimenting with life and that the interest in different belief systems was simply an extension of this ideology.

Apart from the preoccupation with one's religion was the struggle to obtain or retain one's inherent human rights. The mood was right for revolution in the arena; however, one prominent lawyer, Ralph Nader, encouraged irate citizens to channel their energies into a constructive revolt. Nader provided instructional workshops for consumer activists' lawyers and wrote numerous mini-articles and books to assist the consumer in his revolt against private industry. Thus, he won the hearts of many conservatives and liberals alike. Moreover, his philosophy was widely accepted during the 1970's and on into the 1980's.

The heightened impact in human rights and probing analysis of various alleged inequities during the 1960's spurred some women on to organize and revolt against what they labeled as the "traditional double standard". The 1960's created a "me" centered revolution; consequently, traditional roles and ideas were analyzed and modified to conform to the challenging era. This iconoclastic attitude left some American men in a state of confusion and some women in a state of revolution. More women entered the work force with overzealous expectations. Supposedly, some housewives felt stifled and applauded the long awaited renewal of the women's movement.

Some men felt frustrated by the women's movement; consequently, much misunderstanding was initially expressed between the two sexes. Some men felt that the movement was a threat to the traditional male/ female role stratification in society and thus openly resented any reformation. Moreover, some women were uncertain about how the family structure would be changed by the movement; thus, they felt somewhat uneasy.

Undoubtedly, the rising cost of living and subsequent need of additional income created as much of an impetus to seek work as did the movement itself. Concurrent to the rise of women entering the work force was the higher incidence of children enrolled in child care centers. The latter became a sensitive issue in the minds of both men and women as they struggled to give their children the "best".

During your presentations on the 1960's you will want to point out that a multitude of issues perplexed the urbanite besides the women's movement. One of special importance was poverty. Many Middle Americans seemed oblivious to the concern of the poverty stricken. The children, in particular, suffered in the urban areas. Marasmus and kwashiorkor were often seen. Scurvy and rickets also afflicted many in that economic strata, but the permanent physical damage was not as damaging.

However, in 1965 President Johnson signed numerous bills into law, designed to assist the poverty stricken as well as other needy people. These bills were collectively referred to as the Great Society.

The advent of the post-war baby boom from approximately 1945 until 1960 augmented societal concerns. Statisticians of the 1960's era predicted that when that generation of children reached adulthood, the population would ultimately become astronomical. However, many women opted for a career rather than embarking immediately into the role of motherhood. Moreover, from 1965 to 1975, inflation continued spiraling upward which necessitated a two family income.

As stated earlier, inflation was actually a plus to accelerating the women's movement. The overwhelming addition of women into a dominant male work force seemed to be a source of intrigue to the mass media;

hence, the media's coverage somehow gave the movement the credence necessary to succeed.

Because of the dynamic increase in population from 1945-1960, many elementary and secondary schools were constructed in suburbia, designed to ease the prevailing overcrowding condition. Concurrently, many families fled from the rapidly decaying inner city to pollution free suburbia. The majority of persons living in suburbia unconscionably continued to work in the inner city, thus intensifying an already insurmountable citified pollution problem.

You may want to also emphasize during your presentations that the 1960's also produced feelings of great fear, confusion and sadness. The Cuban Missile Crisis produced feelings of apprenhension among many Americans. The Vietnam war produced mixed feelings and served as a dividing force among the youth. The assassinations of President John F. Kennedy, Robert Kennedy and Martin Luther King were particularly disturbing to most Americans. Many Blacks, in particular, were affected by the deaths of King and Malcom X.

King's speeches to the people, which were often indoctrinated with his religious philosophy, promoted a new awakening and controversy among his new found supporters and opponents. "The Speech of 1963" represented the climax of his ministry of peace.

King was instrumental in desegregating the buses in Montgomery, Alabama. In all of his various desegregation campaigns, King stressed the use of nonviolence in achieving the ultimate goal of integration. The various campaigns commenced in the South but eventually disseminated to the Northern states.

His assassination prompted the House of Representatives to enact the Civil Rights Act of 1968. The act clearly delineates the rights of both the American Indian and Black American. Many Blacks and Native Americans felt that the this piece of legislation was long overdue.

While many of the aforementioned 1960 issues initially seemed nebulous to many, the 1970's ultimately provided the clarity and direction needed to place each in its proper perspective. The initial emotive response linked to each issue provided a short lived intensity but instilled a long lived odyssey into the complex solution to each challenging issue.

Focusing on Certain Historical Events and Personalities

Encourage your child to select a historical event or personality to do supplemental research about. You may want to review the last chapter in this book so that if your child asks you questions about methods involved in completing the research, developing the thesis sentence, outlining the research paper, or completing the rough draft, you will have some tips readily available to assist him. Remember, your role is to provide guidance. Sometimes there is a thin line between guidance and interference, and it is difficult to be objective enough at all times to know when you have crossed over the line. However, your child will probably resist by telling you that he can handle the project by himself.

When a child in the 10-12 age group signals to me that he wants to try and tackle the assignment alone, I respect his wishes. Yet I try to be sensitive enough to see that when he becomes frustrated, he needs some assistance. I try to provide the assistance and then proceed to let him continue without interference from me. Remember, that if your child trusts that you will not think that he is foolish or dumb, he will turn to you for assistance. The key is knowing how much and when to assist.

Your child's personality also will enter in to your decision as to when and how often you should assist. When I tutor or teach I adjust my level of assistance so that I won't offend the student's need for self-discovery. Admittedly, this is often difficult; however, if you use a little intuition, you can provide learning experiences that are truly rewarding for your child.

Many documentaries detailing historical events of the 1940's, 1950's and 1960's to name a few are available on videocassettes. So if you own a VCR or have access to one, you may want to contact a librarian at your local library or nearby college library to see if you can rent selected copies. The visualization of what you are presenting will aid your child in comprehending the full impact of the historical event.

If you are presenting a history lesson to more than one child in the 10-12 age group, consider having the children pair off and investigate a historical event or personality jointly. Explain to the children that each pair will be responsible for detailing the event or personality in an oral presentation to the class. Suggest that the students construct visual aids, i.e. graphs, tables, and the like to add interest to the report. Some children may want to dress according to the style of the particular historical era.

Other children may want to focus on the art or music that was popular during that epoch. You may want to request that the children clear the art or music to be presented with you first, so that there won't be any surprises. For example, some of the music that was popular during the 1960's was a little decadent, so you may want to have other suggestions readily available. The movie entitled "The Sound of Music" was quite popular with a cross section of people during the 1960's. Songs from this movie probably would be appealing to many in the class. Obviously, you don't want to censor history; however, you have to be sensitive to the needs of all of the students in the class. Naturally, if you are presenting the history lessons to your child at home, you have the benefit of individualizing the lessons to fit his needs and interests.

Many of my students particularly enjoy learning about the Renaissance period through the study of literature, music and art. Therefore, I have included suggestions on how to present lessons on the Renaissance period in Chapter 5. I also have found that students enjoy studying about ancient history by examining a given civilization's contributions through art, music and literature.

By playing the World Geography Game and presenting oral written reports about historical events which are particularly relevant to him, your child has gained more insight as to where and why certain events transpired. He sees that what has happened in the past has a direct bearing on what may occur in the future. History is no longer inconsequential to him. Foster this interest by encouraging your child or students to read and share information about current events which have some relevance to the subject matter which is being presented. By keeping the spark alive, you will be helping to encourage our next generation of children to be politically aware and active.

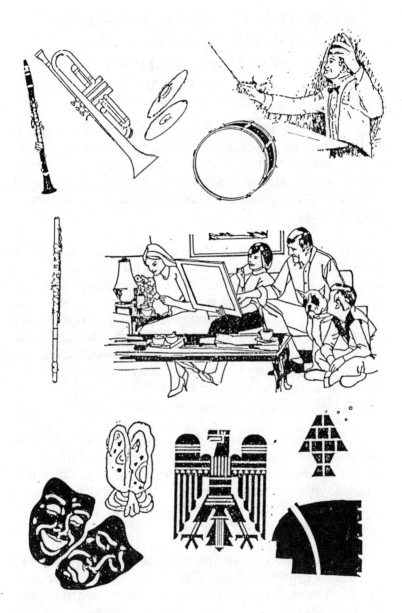

LESSONS IN THE HUMANITIES
FOR FIFTH, SIXTH AND
SEVENTH GRADERS
CHAPTER V

Throughout the ages man has felt the need to express his hopes, dreams and fears. He has used art, music and literature to convey these feelings to members of his community, sometimes giving little thought to the effect his communications would have on future generations.

If your beliefs are derived from a Judeo-Christian philosophy like mine, you will want to stress the importance of not prejudicing beliefs reflected by ancient civilizations. However, during your presentations take time to discuss the myraid of misconceptions expressed by ancient cultures. For example, instead of believing in one true God the Egyptian people believed in many gods. They failed to see the relationship of one supreme being as creator of the universe. Likewise, the ancient Maya belived in various gods.

By comparing two ancient civilizations your child can discover similarities and differences in their belief systems. He can then better appreciate how these ideologies were expressed through the art medium. Moreover, the historical contributions made by these cultures will seem more relevent.

The following example contrasts the art and music of ancient Egypt with the ancient Maya. If you wish to give a presentation on this topic you may want to refer to the books listed in Appendix B. These books will provide you with additional information on these two civilizations so that you can individualize your lesson planning according to your child's interest.

Encourage your child to draw a map of Africa, which illustrates the region occupied by the Egyptians. Likewise, suggest that he also draw a map of Central America and Mexico highlighting the areas occupied by the Aztecs and Maya. Explain that these maps will be useful during your discussions about these civilizations.

Music, Art, and Mythology

An ancient civilization's ideology was often expressed through the intricate binary fusion of music and art which perpetuated the chosen belief or myth. A chosen belief which was endemic to a certain culture often linked the members of the community together, therefore fulfilling their social needs as well. Music and art were simply modes of communication which reinforced cultural beliefs and cemented a sense of togetherness.

In some ancient cultures music was used as a unifying factor. Various chants and ritualistic dances were performed by all members of a culture; thus, a sense of closeness was reinforced. For example, the Maya culture incorporated music into their everyday activities. Ceremonial dances as well as instrumental music were commonplace in the Maya community.

Conversely, some cultures chose art as the primary unifying factor. Music, although important, was not considered as essential as art was. One motivating factor for this choice might be the permanence which the visual mode of communication attempted to elicit. Art was simply a reflection of man's beliefs and attitudes and a continual reminder of his place in the universe. An art object was static, and unlike music, improvisation or change in its original form was considered taboo.

Explain to your child that the ancient Egyptians considered all elements of life to be simply "static". Their comfortable existence which was constantly perpetuated by a predictable climate and fertile soil gave them an almost innate sense of security. Their bountiful supply of food gave them much idle time to record their ideologies on artifacts and create spectacular works of art.

Your child has probably heard about the magnificent pyramids. However, during your presentation you may want to spend time discussing just how these pyramids were constructed. For example, your child will be fascinated to learn that the Egyptians transported by boat more than two million blocks of stone for each of the pyramids built. Naturally, this was a difficult task; therefore, the Egyptians transported the blocks of stone at the time when the Nile River was near or at the flood level stage.

The Great Pyramid of Khufu and the Zoser Pyramid are just two examples of extraordinary works of art left by the ancient Egyptian civilization. During your presentation you may want to mention that the Zoser pyramid represented King Zoser's claim to supreme power as well as the initial unification of the Lower and Upper Kingdoms of Egypt.

The Egyptians paid great homage to the gods of the underworld and appeased them whenever possible. Although the Egyptians never really possessed a truly unified theological system, the general tribute to the deities of the underworld was unanimously acclaimed. The Egyptian "Book of the Dead" artistically documents the belief of the pending journey into the next life through the use of hieratic or hieroglyphic writing. The Egyptians believed that the pharaoh was of paramount importance because he was thought to be the son of

Horus, god of the sun. Thus, great homage was afforded to him. He ruled the people and exerted tremendous control over them.

When the pharaoh died, his body went through an elaborate burial process which would ensure that he would have a successful journey to his next life. Then, he was placed in a highly decorated tomb for his burial. This ritual was performed in accordance with the myth of "Osiris and Isis".

Unfortunately, the Egyptians had difficulty distinguishing between the soul "ka" and man's physical existence. They mistakenly believed that the "ka" of a man could only extend into the heavens (which was simply a celestial archetype of life on earth) by means of a ladder. It was primarily on this premise that the ancient pyramids were constructed.

The Egyptians also considered life to be cyclic rather than linear. This contention was exemplified by the appearance of the sun-disk on various art objects. Re or Ra, the sun-god was the principle deity of worship because of the tremendous life-giving powers he possessed. Thus, during the Vth Dynasty, various sun-temples were erected near the king pyramids.

The Egyptian ideology contrasts sharply with the Maya concept of religion. The Maya believed that the gods would not answer their prayers unless they offered a sacrifice in trade. The Maya, also interestingly enough, often incorporated various aspects of the Aztecs culture into their own cultural activities. Therefore, you may want to encourage your child to read some books about the Aztecs as well.

During your presentation stress that in most ancient civilizations the need to believe in a supreme being fulfilled a quest for identity and gave life an additional dimension of purpose. Visions, dreams and experiences formed an individual's conclusatory images about his earthy surroundings and assisted him in the adjustment of the uncertainty of life after death. Most cultural myths incorporated a moral or a "code of ethics" for the people to live by. The mortal hope for eternal life was promised to those who practiced the chosen moral of the myth, i.e. "set of standards".

In other ancient cultures there was the belief that both animate and inanimate objects possessed a soul. Mana was considered to be a supernatural force which could possibly be embedded in both inanimate and animate objects. A shaman or healer was thought to have some mystical force which enabled him to magically cure the ill. A sacred stone, bowl, totem or inanimate objects could be thought of as magical, and these too were labeled as mana.

Supernatural beings often displayed themselves through anthropomorphic imagery. Explain to your child that celestial bodies, man, reptiles or animals were usually involved in this joint relationship. The Maya belief in the supernatural was particularly interesting.

Emphasize that duality in the Maya theology was clearly illustrated in the Aztecs *Myth of Quetzalcoatl*, lord of life and earth. Quetzalcoatl, literally translated, means plumed water serpent. Although the Maya called Quetzalcoatl by the name KuKulcan, the description of this mythological creature was similar.

Quetzalcoatl was reported to be the color of jade. He represented the earth and water in the form of a serpent as well as representing the sky in the shape of a bird. He was indeed a magical creature to the Aztecs and Maya.

In fact, the Aztecs mistakenly thought that Cortez was Quetzalcoatl because of his physical appearance. According to the Aztec myth, Quetzalcoatl would come to his people by way of the sea. Therefore, when they saw this different appearing gentleman, who arrived by sea, carrying foreign weapons, i.e. guns, they felt he must be Quetzalcoatl.

Both the Egyptian and Mayan cultures interlaced the "like produces like" mythical concept into their mundane existence. The Egyptians painted elegant scenes of a simulated "game hunt" (depicting numerous slaughtered animals) to insure a successful hunt. Likewise, pictorial murals made by the Maya demonstrated their acceptance of this mythical idea.

The ancient Egyptians and Maya used hieroglyphics to communicate with one another. The following pages contain examples of these hieroglyphics and number symbols commonly used by the Egyptians and Maya. These number systems were used for counting rather than for complicated computations.

Comparing Ancient Egyptian and Maya Music

The musical philosophy of the ancient Egyptians drastically differed from the Maya. Music was considered to be a very secular medium in which only a few performers were allowed to participate. The Egyptian "bourgeois" considered group music peasant-like. Secular music was performed only for the elite and mostly on special occasions. Conversely, sacred music was appreciated by the rest of the populace.

The music was primarily monophonic, and because of its oral tradition, there are no traces of the melodies that were performed by these early Maya. Remnants of pictorial murals, however, do give us some clues as to the values the Maya and Egyptians placed on

MAYAN COUNTING

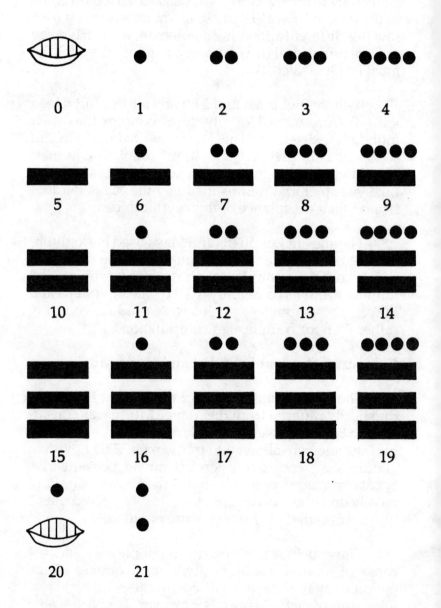

EGYPTIAN NUMBERS

ONE	/	TWO	//
THREE	/ / /	FOUR	/ / / /
FIVE	/ / / / /	SIX	/ / / / / /
SEVEN	/ / / / / / /	EIGHT	/ / / / / / / /
NINE	/ / / / / / / / /	TEN	∩
ELEVEN	∩ /	TWELVE	∩ //
TWENTY	∩ ∩	HUNDRED	⌐
THOUSAND		MILLION	

SOME GLYPHS OF MAYAN TIME PERIOD

TUN
1 YR OF UNALS
360 DAYS

KATUN
20 TUNS
7,200 DAYS

BAKTUN
20 KATANS
144,000 DAYS

PICTUN
20 BAKTUNS
2,880,000 DAYS

CALABTUN
20 PICTUNS
57,600,000 DAYS

KINCHILTUN
20 CALABTUNS
1,152,000,000 DAYS

music. For example, the journey into the next life was accompanied with pictorial murals which depicted various musicians eloquently engaged in performing a melodious piece. Dance, a form of musical expression, was often utilized by the Maya to insure a prosperous hunt or to insure a bountiful crop. Explain that many pictorial murals also artistically express the essence of these ritualistic dances.

During your presentation emphasize that one significant determinant of mythological expression is the constitution and abundance of selected natural resources. The importance of the gem jade is just one example. As you will remember, Quetzalcoatl was described as being the color of jade. Therefore, explain to your child that this myth undoubtedly influenced the spread and utilization of this gem. You may want to mention the following supporting evidence during your presentation. Jade was used in the construction of many of the Maya ceremonial masks. Further mention that jade necklaces and other jade containing artifacts have also been discovered during archaeological excavations.

The Egyptians often embedded ivory as well as other endemic materials into the jewelry which accompanied the departed on his excursion into the next life. Actually, it was the proper consistency of clay with other natural constituents which enabled the architectural structures, sculptures, and so forth to remain permanently affixed. Thus, the "static" myth was perpetuated from generation to generation. It was only from this selective use of endemic natural resources that man could record his thoughts, thereby leaving a clue to the meaning of his myth.

• • •

Refer to Appendix D for a list of books which will be helpful to you when you complete the necessary research for your presentation. You will want to individualize your presentation according to your child's interest in the subject matter. If your child loves to draw you may want to concentrate on presenting a comparative study of Egyptian and Maya art. If your child enjoys the study of geography you may want to underscore the relationship of climate to the development of the belief systems and cultural adaptations. If you want to present this lesson from a Judeo-Christian standpoint, you will want to use **The History of the World in Christian Perspective Volume I by A Beka.** See Appendix B. This book is written on the seventh grade level, so if your child is 11 or 12 he might enjoy reading passages from this text, particularly sections pertaining to Egyptian mythology.

The preparation of lessons on post-medieval, premodern music and art can proceed smoothly if you remember to include the following. Focus your presentations on a single art period, i.e. Renaissance, Baroque, etc. Next, discuss how the societal concerns of that era were reflected in the music, art and literature. Finally, compare the artistic works of this era with the works from previous or subsequent eras. Let's use the Renaissance period as an example.

Lessons on the Renaissance

Beginning early in the 14th century and extending throughout the 16th century humanity went through an intellectual awakening. This period in our history is referred to as the Renaissance, a term meaning "rebirth". As you know, the historical period which preceded the Renaissance was a time of great disillusionment and religious repression. Thus, the Renaissance served to awaken man's interest in the universe, and changes in art, music, and literature reflected this emerging ideology.

By presenting lessons which focus on the art, music and literature of the Renaissance, your child will learn to appreciate the historical significance of this period. Moreover, he will develop skills which will help him to distinguish works of art completed during earlier or later periods. He will also become familiar with the literary giants and the musical greats of the Renaissance.

A Look at Renaissance Art

A child between the ages of 10 and 12 is ready to fully detect the nuances that distinguish one period of art from another. Therefore, much time during your presentation should be spent on classifying works of art according to their respective art periods. This exercise is done in many Montessori schools throughout the United States, and such training can be easily incorporated in a home environment as well.

To prepare for your presentation you will need to purchase ten inexpensive manilla folders, one for each of the ten art periods. The periods of art are as follows:

Byzantine	*(Giotto, Masaccio)*
Renaissance	*(Da Vinci, Michelangelo, Raphael)*
Baroque	*(Rembrandt, El Greco)*
Rococo	*(Gainsborough, Delacroix)*
Impressionism	*(Degas, Monet)*
Neo-Impressionism	*(Van Gogh, Toulouse-Lautrec)*
Cubism	*(Picasso, Matisse)*
Expressionism	*(Klee, Kandinsky)*
Surrealism	*(De Chirico, Ernst)*
Pop Art	*(Blake, Hanson)*

Next, if it's been awhile since you studied art history, you may want to refer to Appendix D for a list of books that will help give you a synopsis as well as examples of the work done by these famous artists. Many museums sell postcards (reproductions) of the artists work which will also be on display in the gallery area. Therefore, you may want to consider writing to inquire as to the cost of postcards which are currently available. Some of the museums do have gift shops and/or bookstores where these postcards are sold. Your friends and relatives living in other states may be able to purchase some of the postcards for you. You may also be able to purchase some of these postcards by mail.

Next, using a few sheets of paper, jot down notes about the Byzantine art period. For instance, you may wish to include that the Byzantine period began around 335 A.D. Distinguishable features included the use of bright, vivid color, and gold was used as a backdrop. Frescos or paintings done on walls were common. There was little dimension. Figures looked rigid. Explain to your child that the rigidness of the figures was consistent with the unyielding religious views of the day.

While you and your child analyze the (reproductions) postcards of this period, encourage your child to note the similarities in style. Discuss in detail the compositions of these paintings. Then, compare them with those of the Renaissance period. When you are finished, place the Byzantine era postcards with notes into a separate folder for later use.

During a subsequent presentation you will want to discuss the contributions made by Renaissance artists. Glance over the postcards which are representative of works done during this period. (I encourage you to purchase the Harper-Trophy set of **Art for Children** books.) For information about these books write to Harper & Row Junior Books, 10 East 53rd Street, New York, NY 10022, or contact **Michael Olaf "The Montessori Shop"** in Arcata, California. (See Appendix C.)

These books beautifully detail the lives of the great artists. They are well written and the text is accompanied by large reproductions of the work done by each artist. Thus, your child has more of an opportunity to revel in the intricacies that make each picture a masterpiece. For your convenience I have listed the complete set.

ART FOR CHILDREN

Renoir	Van Gogh	Gauguin
Da Vinci	Velasquez	Remington
Matisse	Rembrandt	Michelangelo
Klee	Durer	Raphael
Picasso	Chagall	Rousseau
	Toulouse-Lautrec	

Explain to your child that during the Renaissance period an oil-based paint was commonly used. Sometimes the oil-based paint was used with tempera. This yielded a different texture due to the luminous quality associated with oils. Next, ask your child to compare works done during the Renaissance with those completed during the Byzantine. Discuss the differences in the shadings used by Renaissance artists. Emphasize that some artists like Da Vinci incorporated the study of anatomy and mathematics into art. Thus, these paintings have more dimension, and the human figures appear more lifelike.

Religious paintings of the Renaissance also differ from the preceding period. The subjects seem introspective and apprehensive. Perhaps this reflects the religious turmoil apparent during the Renaissance.

Place your notes and postcards (reproductions) pertaining to the Renaissance period in a separate folder.

Next, prepare a third folder for your discussion of the Baroque period. Plan to devote time during your next presentation to comparing the works of the Renaissance and Baroque periods.

Prepare for this presentation by removing the postcards from the Renaissance folder and spreading them out on one side of the table. On the other side of the table, arrange the postcards which are representative of the Baroque period. Next, encourage your child to study the differences as well as the similarities.

Explain that the Baroque style of art flourished beginning in the early 1600's through the mid 1700's. The use of color and light make this period most remarkable. Rembrandt and El Greco, in particular, used the bold, dynamic use of dark and light to capture the emotional intensity of the scenes created.

Rembrant used color and light to create an illusion which almost had a two dimensional effect. The technique of creating the balanced effect of brilliant/dark on the canvas came to be known as **chiaroscuro**. Rembrandt's *The Blinding of Samson*, painted in 1636 and *The Rising of Lazarus*, painted in 1630, are examples of how chiaroscuro was applied. By using this technique Rembrandt brilliantly captured the drama of these biblical events.

El Greco, who may be considered an artist of the High Renaissance / Baroque period, also used color to evoke a spiritual feeling. However, unlike Rembrandt, he often elongated the figures, making his subjects look distorted. Explain to your child that most artists of the Renaissance/Baroque period aspired to create figures that were more lifelike. Thus, El Greco's work was not easily understood. Unlike his colleagues, he seemed determined to incorporate elements of Byzantium art into his paintings.

During subsequent presentations, encourage your child to compare/contrast the Renaissance with the subsequent art periods, i.e. Renaissance/Rococo, Renaissance/Impressionism, Renaissance/Neo-Impressionism, Renaissance/Cubism, Renaissance/Expressionism, Renaissance/Surrealism and Renaissance/ Pop Art. By keeping notes and postcards for each period in separate folders, your child can periodically do this exercise either with you or at times alone.

I suggest that each subsequent period be contrasted with the Renaissance in sequence so that your child can see how the styles of art have evolved. He will also discover how artists have incorporated elements from the various periods into their own compositions. Such an exercise is believed by many Montessorians to help the child discern and appreciate the role art plays in our society.

Lessons on Renaissance Literature

Understanding literature is a challenge for many students. Often, reading a synopsis of the book sparks enough interest so that the student wants to read the book in its entirety. Therefore, to encourage interest in literature, particularly the classics, I highly recommend the **Illustrated Classics** by Pendulum Press. Many of these books are mentioned in **Modern Montessori at Home;** however, I have found that fifth, sixth and seventh graders also enjoy reading through these classics. Later, the student may decide to visit the library with the purpose of borrowing not only the principal book that initially peaked his interest but additional books written by the same author as well.

While at the library, encourage your child to borrow *Shakespeare for Children*, written by **Cass Foster**. This book gives children of all ages a delightful introduction to the world of Shakespeare. See Appendix A for additional information about the *Illustrated Classics* and *Shakespeare for Children*.

William Shakespeare was one of the literary giants that emerged during the Renaissance period. Therefore, it's only fitting that your presentations include an insight into how history was reflected in his plays. Prepare for your presentations by reading the Shakespeare plays in their entirety. **Some** of the plays, particularly *MacBeth*, may be too sanguineous for many fifth, sixth and seventh graders, so I usually avoid recommending them. Children at this age are often impressionable and I feel many can't fully appreciate *MacBeth* until they are more mature.

You may want to consider preparing a lesson about *Romeo & Juliet* or *Julius Caesar*. For example, if you present a lesson on *Julius Caesar* you might consider using the following as an example.

First, encourage your child to read the **Pendulum Press** version of *Julius Caesar*. Next, encourage him to read pages 194-243 in the **A Beka** *Masterpieces from World Literature*. See Appendix B.

Background Information for Initial Presentation

Explain to your child that most of the Shakespearean plays incorporated the hopes and fears which exemplified the Elizabethan era. Therefore, historical symbolism permeates throughout the plays and provides the viewer or reader with a glimpse of 16th century European life. Soliloquies, dreams, soothsayers, ghosts and other forms of symbolism are employed in an eloquent although inconspicuous manner. During the presentation emphasize that Shakespeare's insertion of symbolism into the playscript was always deliberate.

Emphasize that Julius Caesar is portrayed as a true statesman and humanitarian. Further explain that around 79 B.C. rivals Ginaeus Popeius, (Pompey), and Julius Caesar aspired to gain control of Rome. Pompey wanted the aristocracy to rule, while Caesar opted to give the common people more of an opportunity to participate in governmental affairs.

For awhile, Caesar was the victor. The common people were initially delighted with the many reforms that were instituted during his reign. Statues were erected in his honor; the month Quintilis was changed to Julius, and coins bore his icon. Needless to say, Julius felt powerful and became somewhat prideful. Some felt intimated by the power he possessed and were afraid that he might designate himself as the king.

Consequently, plots were underway to rid Rome of this would be tyrant. Marcus Junius Brutus and his fellow conspirator Gaius Cassius Longinus schemed to overthrow Julius Caesar, and the play spotlights the motives and actions of these supporting characters. Actually, Julius Caesar is not the hero of this play; Brutus is.

Emphasize that the thesis of this play deals with how to best rid Rome of tyranny. Ultimately, Caesar becomes targeted and he meets with death on March 15th, commonly referred to as the Ides of March.

Brutus and Cassius – The Conspirators

Explain that Brutus is unsatisfied with the state of public affairs and is also dissatisfied with the chain of events in his own life. Discuss with your child that although Brutus plots against his rival Julius, he initially befriends him. Of course, as you'll remember, his shrewd friend, Cassius, goads him on to kill Julius.

Cassius portrays the supreme schemer. He manipulates Brutus in much the same manner as Lady MacBeth handles her husband. At this point in your presentation you may want to compare/contrast the character qualities of Brutus and Cassius. Emphasize that Cassius is more perceptive than Brutus. He has an uncanny ability of knowing just what to say at the appropriate moment. He is cerebral and unemotional. Unlike Caesar, he is not superstitious; thus, he finds no need for concern when an unnatural storm arises as described in Act I, Scene 3. Instead, seeing that supporting characters like Cinna and Casca are unnerved by such an event, he decides to take advantage of the situation by steering the topic of conversation in another direction, e.g. the overthrow of Roman tyranny.

Like MacBeth, Julius Caesar, is a combination of the classical Greek and Elizabethan tragic hero. For example, both Caesar and Brutus suffer guilt from being prideful. Moreover, Julius Caesar's and Brutus' actions somewhat determine the ultimate outcome. However, you will want to mention to your child that while the soothsayer warns Julius Caesar of his ultimate fate, it is the ghost of Julius which haunts Brutus.

Brutus is plagued by the ghost of Julius throughout the play. Emphasize that in Act V, Scene 5 when Brutus is anticipating defeat he begs his men to kill him. Finally, as you'll remember one of them consents, and on Brutus' dying lips, he murmurs, "Caesar now be still, I killed not thee with half so good a will." Thus, the symbolism of guilt proves to be as tragic in a drama as it can be in real life.

Shakespeare's plays often reflected the struggle between good and evil which faced the 16th century man. During this era man was consumed by his place in the universe. He believed that God created the world and there was the temptation to question God's existence or ignore God's place in the scheme of things which created conflict. Thus, the conflicts in Shakespeare's plays revealed the struggles his heroes and heroines felt when they challenged or disregarded their God given positions in life.

A suggested supplemental exercise that many of my students seem to enjoy involves selecting one favorite character from the play and analyzing him or her. Encourage your child to write a two page essay about the strengths and weaknesses of the chosen character. Your child may want to answer the following questions in his essay so that the reader is able to better appreciate the character.

1. *What qualities attracted you to this character?*
2. *Was he a passive observer or was he the organizer and/ or aggressor?*
3. *How did his behavior affect the other characters in the play? Was he manipulative? Were his actions towards others covert or overt?*
4. *What mistakes, if any, do you think this character made?*
5. *What advice, if any, would you have offered to this character?*
6. *Do you think that this character would be a good friend? Support your answer by stating why or why not.*

Another supplemental exercise which I am sure that your child will be familiar with is the construction of a time line. Time lines are an excellent means of organizing events in a chronological order. You may want to encourage your child to include all artists, musicians, and literary giants of the Renaissance era on a single time line. Alternatively, your child may select to make a time line for each discipline, i.e. listing all artists of the Renaissance period on a single time line, musicians on another time line, and so forth.

Other works by Renaissance authors are listed for your convenience. These works also represent the prevailing attitudes that were expressed during this period in our history.

RENAISSANCE AUTHORS

Miguel de Cervantes   *Don Quixote*
Moliere   *The Misanthrope*
John Milton   *Paradise Lost*
John Bunyan   *Pilgrim's Progress*
Daniel Defoe   *Robinson Crusoe*
Rene Descartes   *Discourse on Method*
Francis Bacon   *The New Atlantis*

Lessons on Renaissance Music

In order for your child to fully appreciate the style and compositional qualities which make the Renaissance music distinct you will need to acquaint your child with some basic music terminology. Moreover, extensive listening is required for music to be fully appreciated. As you know, unlike art, music is not a visual medium. Therefore, I strongly recommend that you obtain the following materials for your presentations. Check first with your local library, to see if you can borrow these items. If not, you can purchase the items from the following distributors.

In Print for Children
Orchestral Instruments
Classification Cards

Instruments of the Symphony
Orchestra Poster

Young Discovery Library
Music!
(Also available through **Michael Olaf, The Montessori Shop**)

The Moss Music Group, Inc.
The Music Master Series
Their Stories & Music
Cassette Tape Series
(Also available through **Michael Olaf, The Montessori Shop**)

Prokofiev Peter & The Wolf
Britten Young Person's Guide to the Orchestra
(Also available through **Michael Olaf, The Montessori Shop**)

During your first presentation familiarize your child with the instruments of the orchestra. With the packet of the *Orchestral Instruments Classification* cards in hand, demonstrate how the cards are classified according to category, i.e. woodwind, string, and so on. Next, shuffle the cards and encourage your child to line the cards up under the appropriate section, i.e. pictures of the wood wind instruments go under the wood wind category, the brass instruments go under the brass category and so forth. During the remainder of the presentation, encourage your child to listen to Side 2 of the Britten's *Young Person's Guide to the Orchestra*. Your child will then be familiar with the sound made by each of the instruments.

Next, encourage your child to read *Music!* in its entirety. Your child will discover the answers to questions like: What are the three families of the instruments? What were the first woodwinds made of? What are the parts of the violin? The **Young Discovery Books** are well recognized and appreciated by educators in this country. The publishers have been recipients of numerous awards for their contributions to excellence in education. These books are beautifully illustrated; thus, your child is bound to exhibit much enthusiasm after reading *Music!* He will probably be anxious to read other books in the **Young Discovery** series as well.

During a subsequent learning session you will want to present your child with some new terms which will help him to better appreciate classical music. Thus, if it's been awhile since you studied music or you just want to review all aspects of music so that you will be better prepared for your next presentation, I recommend reading books mentioned in Appendix D. In particular, you will want to review the following terms: Homophony, polyphony, counterpoint, motets, madrigals, chamber music and fugues.

As previously mentioned, the arts were profoundly affected by the emerging ideas of the Renaissance. Like Renaissance art and literature, music underwent a revolution which became even more apparent during the subsequent Baroque period. Three-part polyphony flourished during the mid-Renaissance period. Explain to your child that polyphonic music is rather difficult to listen to at first, because of the demands placed upon the listener.

Present a lesson about polyphony by using a three-part polyphonic piece. Using a three-part polyphonic piece as an example, explain that the listener must listen for three distinct voices. If you sing and/or read music you are very familiar with the parts written for different voices, i.e. soprano, alto, bass and the like. Therefore, as your child initially listens to the three-part polyphonic piece, encourage him to concentrate his attention upon the soprano voice. The next time the piece is played, request that he listen for the alto voice. Finally, during the third listening encourage him to concentrate on the bass voice. Guillaume de Machaut, G.P. da Palestrina and Josquin des Prez used polyphony extensively; thus, for listening purposes; you may want to inquire at your local library as to the availability of records featuring these musical artists.

Giovanni Pierluigi da Palestrina's *"Pope Marcellus Mass"* is just one example how polyphony was used to create a majestic masterpiece. Suggest that your child listen to a recording of *"Pope Marcellus Mass"* four times. First, encourage him to listen to the soprano voice. Next, suggest that he listen to the alto voice. During the third period of listening he should concentrate on the tenor voice. Finally, during the fourth repetition of this piece he should focus his listening on the bass voice.

This a cappella version has a stirring effect upon the listener. Palestrina did this deliberately. He wanted to create a musical piece which would cause the listener to reflect upon his relationship with God. The a cappella effect (without accompaniment) is significant in that it heightens the emotional impact of the piece. The listener's attention is not diverted; thus, he can direct his thoughts inward and contemplate deeper spiritual matters.

Palestrina, who was born circa 1525 in Rome and died in 1594, was considered to be one of the most highly regarded musicians of this mid-Renaissance period. He was a prolific composer. He is credited with writing at least 245 motets, numerous madrigals, hymns and so on. Like many of his colleagues, Palestrina wrote exclusively for the voice.

Explain to your child that orchestral music was not commonplace during the Renaissance era. The bass and treble recorder, viols, lute and organ were some of the instruments used to entertain guests during festivals or other social gatherings. Moreover, chamber music was very popular during this era. Emphasize that the terms chamber music and ensemble are synonymous. The ensemble was composed of two to twelve players; each player was assigned a part of like value. Further explain that the string quartet which originated during the mid-1700's is an example of chamber music heard today.

(The string quartet consists of two violins, a viola and a cello.) Thus, early chamber music which was pleasing and in constant demand during the Renaissance and post-Renaissance period is still appreciated by audiences of the 1990's.

Another eminent composer of the Renaissance period was Josquin des Prez, who lived circa 1440-1495. Like Palestrina, des Prez used contrapuntal techniques (polyphony) to create religious masterpieces. Although his compositions had the reverent quality which was a trademark of religious Renaissance music, he managed to add embellishments, particularly ones which yielded a harmonic effect. His motets of *Ave Maria* are excellent examples of his ingenuity. If possible, borrow a recording of one of des Prez's *Ave Marias* at your local library. (If you live close to a state university library, you may want to inquire as to the possibility of borrowing a tape or record of des Prez's *Ave Marias* from the humanities section of the library.)

Madrigals and Motets

Madrigals were written for secular occasions. These poetic polyphonic musical pieces were sung to small groups; the beautiful madrigal music added much to the festivities. Conversely, the motet was created for the Catholic service.

Palestrina vs. des Prez

During a subsequent presentation encourage your child to listen to works of Palestrina and des Prez. Ask him to comment upon the similarities and differences that seem apparent to him. Reiterate that both Palestrina and des Prez used polyphony while many Medieval composers of religious music initially used monophony. Stress that polyphony was an outgrowth of monophony. The Gregorian chant was used during the Medieval period in the Catholic ceremony. Further explain that the Gregorian chant, or plainsong as it was sometimes referred to, consisted of one melodic line. It was not accompanied by any other voice or instrument.

Comparing the Renaissance with the Baroque Period

Music of the subsequent Baroque period was filled with much polyphony; however, there was a new accent on homophonic texture. Explain to your child that this homophonic music consisted of one melodic line with accompanying harmony.

During the Baroque era composers like Bach used tempo notations to indicate how music should be played. For example, terms like *adagio* meaning slowly, and *allegro*, meaning lively tempo were used. These notations helped the musician interpret and play the music with the feeling intended.

As in the art world, the music world of the Baroque period also witnessed other elaborate changes. These innovative ideas reflected the monumental changes which were escalating in society during this period. As an extension of Renaissance ideology, musicians of the Baroque period were encouraged rather than discouraged to pursue artistic expression.

The seeds that were nourished during the Renaissance realized fruition during the Baroque period. For example, the chorale, overture, opera and sonata are just some examples of how creative sparks introduced during the Renaissance laid the foundation for these musical concepts to materialize.

During the Baroque period the fugue was used extensively. Bach, considered a master of the fugue, used this musical form to create many intricate patterns in his musical compositions. Emphasize that a fugue starts by introducing a thesis. This rather plain melody orients the listener to the primary theme. The primary theme or exposition is followed by a series of various voices which answer or restate this primary theme, *Bach's Toccata and Fugue in D minor, S. 565,* and *Passacaglia and Fugue in C minor, S. 582, are ideal* examples of how Bach mastered the art of the fugue. Listen and discuss these musical pieces with your child. The two of you may want to borrow additional recordings of Bach's works; consequently, the reference librarian at your local library will be happy to direct you to additional recordings that your child will enjoy listening to.

Supplemental Readings

The following books will greatly aid your child in understanding and appreciating the artistic contributions of the masters of the Renaissance and Baroque periods.

Ladybird Books
The Story of the Theatre
Discovering Shakespeare Country
Lives of the Great Composers Book 1
Great Artists Book 1
Great Artists Book 2

Additional information about these **Ladybird Books** may be found in Appendix A. These books are beautifully illustrated and the text is detailed enough to satisfy your child's curiosity about many of the masters of the Renaissance and Baroque historical periods. You may want to preview these books first, so that you and your child can discuss these artists in detail during your presentations.

By studying Renaissance art, music and literature your child has become familiar with the vast contributions which were accomplished during a relatively short span of time. He now realizes that a positive, open attitude about learning encouraged rather than discouraged learning in all areas, i.e. art, music, literature, science, religion and so forth. He sees the relationship between historical events and humanitarian contributions. By studying the humanities he learns the importance mankind places upon artistic expression.

LESSONS IN ENGLISH COMPOSITION AND GRAMMAR FOR FIFTH, SIXTH AND SEVENTH GRADERS CHAPTER VI

The lessons throughout this book have been designed to help your child to fully comprehend and appreciate the subject matter that is being presented. Much emphasis has been placed on encouraging your child to write essays, book reports or compositions about particular events or issues on which he would like to further study in-depth. Therefore, this chapter is designed to give you suggestions on how you can assist your child in developing better writing skills.

Modern Montessori at Home deals extensively with elementary grammar and composition. Therefore, if you feel that your child might benefit from a review of the basic fundamentals of grammar and composition, I suggest that you borrow a copy of **Modern Montessori at Home** from your local library before proceeding on to the intermediate grammar and compositional exercises included in this chapter. Only a brief summation of basic grammar and composition will be provided in this chapter; a detailed discussion on these subjects may be found in **Modern Montessori at Home.**

English composition and grammar need not be presented in a vacuum. You can easily incorporate concepts of English composition after you have given a presentation on another academic subject. Let's suppose that you have decided to present a lesson on comparing the religious revolution of the 1960's with the 1740's and that you have given your child an essay question to answer. This would provide an excellent setting to review the steps in planning a paragraph.

Explain to your child that there are three steps in planning a paragraph. These steps include: 1. Selecting an ideas, 2. Choosing a subject, 3. Narrowing the subject. Explain that an idea comprises many thoughts. From this idea one particular subject comes into focus. Next, emphasize that the subject is scaled down or made narrower by deleting thoughts which do not pertain to the subjects.

You may want to use the following to further emphasize the process of the three step plan.

Let's suppose that your want to write about a football game that you recently saw. You would write:
Football game
(outstanding defensive plays)
(touchdowns)
(injuries)

Or, let's suppose that you wanted to consider writing about a school club.
School club
(election of officers)
(guest speakers)
(field trips)

You now have made the decision to write about your school club. Therefore, you need to focus your attention upon the following *ideas*. **(Election of Officers), (Guest Speakers), and (Field Trips).** Now, you must select one of the topics. Let's suppose that you have chosen the topic of (guest speakers).

Now, scale down this topic. Pose questions about the topic which you can answer in your paragraph. Formulate questions which only refer to the topic being discussed. Let's use the following as an example:

1.   *Did you like the guest speaker?*
2.   *What did he or she talk about?*
3.   *How did the students react?*

Next, using a sheet of paper or index card prepare to jot down some notes. Start by answering the questions you formulated about the subject. In the example given above you might respond by indicating that you liked the guest speaker but you found his speech to be boring. Conversely, if you liked the speech you would elaborate and indicate why you found the speech to be interesting. You might also consider including the reaction of the other students. *Were they bored? Did they ask a lot of questions?*

Look over the notes that you have made. Study them carefully. Select a topic sentence. Remember, a topic sentence states the primary idea of the paragraph.

FOR EXAMPLE:

Mrs. Jones, our guest speaker, presented one of the most fascinating viewpoints on the cause of the dinosaurs demise that I had ever heard.

All of the supporting sentences in the paragraph relate to that topic sentence.

FOR EXAMPLE:

Roger, our science club president, recently scheduled a scientist to speak to our club members. Mrs. Jones, our guest speaker, presented one of the most fascinating viewpoints on the cause of the dinosaurs demise that I had ever heard. She talked to our class for one hour, and I guess the other students were fascinated too, because she stayed an additional hour and answered many questions from enthusiastic students.

Notice that each sentence represents a complete thought. Each sentence augments the idea presented in the topic sentence. Moreover, notice how the sentences

in the paragraph answer the questions written on the
sheet of paper or an index card.

1. Did you like the guest speaker?
The person writing the paragraph liked the guest speaker.

2. What did he (she) talk about?
The guest speaker spoke about the cause of the demise
of the dinosaurs.

3. How did the students react?
The students were enthusiastic.

Encourage your child to use this technique when
he answers the essay questions that you pose. For
example, let's suppose that you asked your child to
briefly answer the following essay question? *What
roles did Jonathan Edwards and George Whitefield
play in the "Great Awakening"?*

Typically, a student in the fifth or sixth grade
would write the following.

The Great Awakening created a lot of turmoil
among the American colonies. George Whitefield toured
the country on horse and delivered sermons on the need
for salvation. His counterpart, Jonathan Edwards, also
practiced and preached the same philosophies. In
addition, Edwards believed that one must have an
emotional and spiritual experience in order to actually be
saved. As a result, many churches became divided and
the different sects realized the need to educate upcom-
ing ministers. Consequently, colleges like Princeton for
the Presbyterians and Brown for Baptists were estab-
lished to meet these differing needs.

Writing Reports

When you assign reports, i.e. book reports or research reports, you will want to take time during the end
of your presentations to review the compositional

components which need to be included. Thus, you may want to incorporate the following into your presentations.

First, remind your child that every report has a beginning, where a thesis is presented to the reader, a middle, which consists of one or more paragraphs supporting the thesis, and an ending, where the original thesis is restated and a conclusion is given.

Often, an outline is used to assist in the organization of the report. **The traditional outline is as follows:**

I.   Main Topic
     A. Supporting topic which relates to main topic
     B. Supporting topic which relates to main topic

II. Second Main Topic (like the first Main Topic, the Second Topic supports or relates to the thesis presented in some way)
     A. Supporting topic which relates to second main topic
        1. Additional detail to supporting topic **A**
        2. Additional detail to supporting topic **A**
     B. Supporting topic which relates to second main topic
        1. Additional detail to supporting topic **B**
        2. Additional detail to supporting topic **B**

Remind your child that if he lists **A** under a main topic he must also always list **B**. Moreover, if he lists **1.** under supporting topics **A** or **B** he must also list **2.** In the example above notice that **A** is followed by **B** and **1** is followed by **2.**

Now, let's analyze the following outline done by a typical sixth grader.

ROMEO AND JULIET

I. Ongoing feud between the Capulets and Montagues
    A. Sampson and Gregory, servants of the Capulets
       start fight with the Montagues' servants.
    B. Benvolio intervenes.
    C. Tybalt challenges Benvolio to a duel.
    D. Citizens of Verona now become involved.
    E. Prince Escalus of Verona arrives.

II. Romeo proclaims his love.
    A. Benvolio questions Romeo about his strange
       behavior.
    B. Romeo reveals to Benvolio that he is in love,
       but the girl does not love him.
    C. Benvolio encourages him to find someone else.

III. In the Capulet household there is talk of marriage.
    A. Juliet's mother encourages Juliet to get married.
       1. She reminds Juliet that girls much
          younger are marrying.
       2. She reveals that Count Paris, who wants
          to marry Juliet, will be at the Capulet feast.

IV. This part of the story uses symbolism to reveal
    what the outcome will be.
    A. Foreboding dreams reveal that tragedy will
       cloud any happiness.
    B. Joy for Romeo would only be transitory.
    C. Romeo still plans to attend the Capulet feast,
       nevertheless.

V. The Feast
    A. Musicians play while guests danced, ate and
       talked.
       1. Romeo looks for his true love.
       2. Instead, his eyes fix on one even more
          beautiful.
       3. He falls madly in love with Juliet.
    B. Juliet, too, feels Romeo is special.
       1. She thinks no more of Count Paris.
       2. She and Romeo speak of their love for
          each other.

This outline is well organized. However, the young writer made the mistake of writing complete sentences rather than phrases to express his ideas. Emphasize that sentences are not necessary. (Your child may find this difficult to believe, since he has been encouraged to write complete thoughts for some time now.) However, this outline is meant to organize thoughts, so phrases will suffice. Explain that when the actual composition is written, these phrases will be transformed into sentences by your child.

Now, let's skip to the end of this writer's outline to see how a few simple improvements have made his outline even more organized and concise.

XI   Romeo's fate
    A. Benvolio pleads Romeo's case
    B. Montague speaks of events leading up to Tybalt's death
    C. Prince makes decision
       1. Romeo must leave Verona
       2. If caught before leaving, Romeo will die

XII. Juliet's wedding
    A. Juliet's parents force marriage to Count Paris
    B. Juliet refuses
    C. Plans escapes
    D. Does not reveal marriage to Romeo

XIII. Dramatic death scene
    A. Friar Laurance helps Juliet
       1. Offers her potion
       2. Juliet drinks potion
          a. She will be in deep sleep
          b. She won't have to marry Count Paris
    B. Romeo hears of Juliet's death
       1. Sees Juliet's tomb
       2. Fights with Count Paris near tomb
    C. Romeo swallows poison and dies

D. Juliet awakens
 1. Finds Count Paris and Romeo dead
 2. Proceeds to kill herself with Romeo's dagger
E. The Funeral
 1. Somber mood
 2. Montagues and Capulets see senselessness in fighting
 3. Two families agree to live in peace

Your child may also wish to do in-depth research on a famous personality. Encourage him to give the reader a clear picture by organizing the report as follows: 1. The Setting, i.e. delineating the time and place where this historical figure lived, 2. Characters, i.e. principal people who were important in the historical figure's life, 3. Accomplishments, i.e. awards and prizes given to this historical figure, 4. The Price of Success, i.e. sacrifices the historical figure may have made during his career.

The following example is typical of a sixth or seventh grader's work.

MADAME CURIE

Setting

Marie Curie lived during very turbulent times. She was born on November 7, 1867 and was named Manya Sklodovski by her loving parents. Because she was the youngest, she received much attention from her parents. Manya or Marie as she was later called, grew up in the Russian occupied country of Poland. Marie, like many Poles, took great pride in her country.

The children were instructed not to learn about the history of customs of Poland, but in secret, Marie and her classmates learned much about their Polish heritage. The children spent class time learning domestic skills like sewing, but the teacher also spent much time teaching the children Polish history. Although this was considered a crime by the Russians, the children loved to learn these history lessons.

The teacher had placed much trust in a warning system, a bell, which rang and warned both the teacher and class that Russian officials were about to enter the classroom. The students would hurriedly take out their sewing materials and act as though they were busy learning about the art of sewing.

On one day, in particular, the Russian officials entered the classroom and began to question Marie. They asked her many questions about the czars who had ruled since Catherine II. They asked her to recite many other things as well. Marie was exhausted at the end of the interrogation. After the officials left, Marie burst into tears.

Characters

Marie's mother was a warm, tender, loving person, but Marie felt that her mother always kept Marie at a safe distance. She never was kissed by her mother, and as a child she couldn't understand why this was so. Later, Marie was to find out that her mother was suffering from tuberculosis, and the reason she didn't kiss her daughter was because she didn't want to give Marie the disease.

Like Marie's mother, Marie's father was brilliant. Marie admired the genius of her father. He was very interested in science. He encouraged Marie's interest in science.

Marie's sister, Bronya, was intelligent and through encouragement from Marie and their father, Bronya became a doctor. The Sklodovska children, for the most part, were brilliant, but no one in the family realized how special or unique Marie really was. Marie, herself, didn't realize that she was a genius until she was about 25 years of age.

Marie was a very special person. Her family and her country were the most important things in her life. She was an idealist when she was young. She wanted very much to serve her country. She also wanted to serve her family as best as she could.

She worked as a tutor to help her sister Bronya through medical school. She also helped with her father's expenses. Although she sometimes hated the tutoring jobs, she was committed to helping her family. She put her personal feeling aside.

This wasn't always easy. For example, while she was employed as a governess for a wealthy family, she fell in love with the eldest son who often came home for visits from college. He asked her to marry him, and she very much wanted to do so. His family was opposed to such a marriage taking place because they felt that Marie was beneath them. Marie swallowed her pride and continued working there as a tutor. She vowed that she would never let love interfere in her life again.

Accomplishments

Marie was often the best in her class. For example, when she graduated from high school in June 1883 she received the gold medal for being the best student in the class. She also received recognition as best in her class at Sorbonne. Because Marie was fluent in so many languages she could study in various countries; and France was one of her favorites. Later, Marie received the Nobel Prize. She shared this prize with Henri Becquerel, the man who was responsible for the theory of radioactivity. Finally, in 1921, Marie and her daughters received a gift of radium from President Harding of the United States.

The Price of Success

Marie spent many long hours doing research in science. Finally, she met a man, Pierre Curie, who shared her love for science. At last, Marie could communicate with someone who was on her level. Pierre seemed to understand how important her research projects were to her. He shared her interest in isolating the component which radiated. Because the component radiated, Marie named it radium.

Radium became important for mankind. It was used in World War I to help doctors diagnose by X-ray which bones were fractured. Marie spent many long hours out in the battlefield helping the doctors use the radium properly so that they could make accurate diagnoses and save many lives.

It seemed that everyone wanted radium, but, Marie and her husband Pierre were humanitarians. They didn't want to make a profit. They just wanted to help mankind. They decided to share their knowledge with all.

At a time when everything seemed to be going so well for Marie, tragedy struck. Pierre was killed in a horrible accident. He accidently stepped off a curb and a team of horses crushed him. Marie now was left alone to raise two daughters, Irene and Eve. She took this job very seriously and was a good mother to the girls.

Unfortunately, all of the experiments Marie Curie did with radium ultimately caused her death. She died of radium poisoning on July 4, 1934. She suffered from aplastic pernicious anemia which probably was a result of injured bone marrow by a long accumulation of radiations. She left a legacy to mankind, however. This legacy will live on forever.

During a learning session you and your child may want to review "Madame Curie" together. Emphasize the first paragraph under the heading SETTING is well organized. The last sentence in this paragraph is an excellent example of how to correctly use a transitional sentence. This sentence encourages the reader to now focus on Marie's early learning about her country. The next two paragraphs contain interesting sentences which all support or relate to the topic being discussed.

Now, direct your child's attention to the first paragraph listed under the heading CHARACTERS. This young writer wrote a very eloquent account of Marie's relationship with her mother. However, the final sentence in this paragraph is a bit awkward and does not represent a good transitional sentence into the next topic being presented. Likewise, the next paragraph contains three rather choppy sentences. Whenever possible, encourage your child to use transitional words like nevertheless, moreover, furthermore, similarly, consequently, therefore, and so on to join phrases together. Stress that transitional words help the reader to fully appreciate and comprehend the ideas that are being presented.

Demonstrate that by using a few transitional words the sentences are smoothly connected. This yields a clearer picture of what the writer is attempting to communicate to the reader.

FOR EXAMPLE:
Marie admired the genius of her father. He was very interested in science. He encouraged Marie's interest in science. (**BECOMES**) Marie admired the genius of her father. He was very interested in science, and he understood Marie's fascination with learning as much as she could about it. Therefore, he encouraged Marie's interest in science. Encouragement, after all, was a trait that one Sklodovski always gave to one another.

The last sentence helps to connect the thoughts from this paragraph with the subsequent paragraph which introduces information about Bronya.

131

Under the heading ACCOMPLISHMENTS we see that this young writer had some difficulties in the first paragraph. Stress that the following sentence connects two ideas that should not be joined together with the conjunction **and** because the ideas really don't relate to one another. This sentence reads as follows: **Because Marie was fluent in so many languages she could study in many different countries, and France was one of her favorites.** Emphasize that conjunctions like and, or, nor and the like must only be used to join ideas that relate to one another.

Now, direct your child's attention to the last paragraph under the heading THE PRICE OF SUCCESS. This last paragraph is typical of how many young writers wind up the report. (QUICK AND INCOMPLETE). Stress that the summation need not be lengthy; however, the reader's curiosity about the subject he has been exposed to should be somewhat satisfied. New information presented in the summation paragraph only baffles and frustrates the reader. It does not satisfy him.

Obviously, additional information was presented in the summation paragraph about Marie Curie, but this does not detract from the report. The reader realizes that Marie Curie has died. However, it would have been more appropriate to present this information in the next to the last paragraph.

The last paragraph should have dealt exclusively with the legacy that Marie Curie left. Her accomplishments and contributions should have been restated. Then the reader would have felt more satisfied. **This legacy will live on forever.** This is a good ending sentence; however, if the legacy had been restated for the reader, the reader would have been reminded of the impact this historical figure made upon society and on the reader's life in particular.

132

The preparation and writing that goes into a review may provide another excellent means for your child to learn more about the arts while perfecting his compositional skills. For example, you may want to encourage your child to attend a classical music concert, a play, or a musical production and write about his impressions of what he saw and heard. Moreover, a **review** provides an excellent opportunity for your child to associate new terms which were introduced during the presentations with what he hears and sees on the stage. Notice how the terms *allegro, andante,* and *presto* were used by the young writer in the following review. Please note that the dates and places may have been changed in the following reviews:

MY FAIR LADY

On Tuesday evening, February 24th, the Long Beach Civic Light Opera Association presented its opening night version of *"My Fair Lady"*. The production was held at the Jordan Theatre which is adjacent to Jordan High School in the city of Long Beach.

After approximately a 20 minute delay, the overture of *"My Fair Lady"* began. The overture conveyed the lyrical form which predominated throughout the entire score. A concise introduction preceded the overture and eloquently introduced a medley of "You Did It", "On the Street Where You Live" and "I Could Have Dance All Night". The tempo throughout the overture was allegro. There were slight tempo changes between the transitions varying from andante to presto.

The orchestra naturally maintained a low profile throughout the evening with a few minor exceptions. The bassoon highlighted many comical moments, especially in Scenes I through III in Act I. The percussion came to the forefront on occasion. One occasion was in the "Rain in Spain" when a mock bullfight dance was performed. The tambourine and castanets especially accented the delightful Latin rhythm and greatly added to the visualization of the scene.

Homophony dominated most of the score. Polyphony was introduced briefly in the second stanza of "I Could Have Danced All Night" and added a pleasant diversion in texture. The musical score was pleasant and lyrical with only a few sharp angulations apparent to the listener. This, of course, isn't surprising when one stops and analyzes the particular style of Frederick Loewe and Alan Jay Lerner.

I personally feel that this distinct style has contributed to the continuous success of such hits as "Gigi", "Camelot", "Paint Your Wagon", and of course "My Fair Lady". By the reaction of this audience, I think that many will certainly agree. This definitely was demonstrated by the Long Beach Civic Light Opera on its opening night of this successful musical.

Notice that in this second review that the writer compares a Mendelssohn concerto with a Beethoven concerto. Thus, he demonstrates that through extensive listening he has learned to differentiate between different techniques and styles used by the different composers.

SYMPHONIES FOR YOUTH

On April 29th, the Los Angeles Philharmonic presented a "Symphonies for Youth" concert.. The concert was held at the Music Center Pavilion. The program consisted of six exceptionally gifted teenage musicians, each performing an excerpt of a selected compositional piece. The compositions included: Beethoven's Piano Concerto No. 3 in C minor, Op. 37 - Third Movement, Mozart's Violin Concerto in G, K.216 - Third Movement, Capuzzi's Concerto in F for Double Bass - First Movement, Bruch's Violin Concerto No. 1 in G minor - First

Movement, Medelssohn's Piano Concerto No. 1 in G minor-Third Movement and Beriot's Scene de Ballet.

The climax of the program was the stupendous performance of fourteen year old Tom Segal. Segal's interpretation of Medelssohn's Piano Concerto No. 1 in G minor Third Movement was exhilarating. The audience demonstrated its approval by giving the young performer a standing ovation.

Mendelssohn's concerto spotlights the pianist's ability and in doing so creates a certain assertive fluidity over the orchestral accompaniment. In contrast, Beethoven's Piano Concerto No. 3 in C minor sharply contrasts with Mendelssohn's concept. The piano is used a device which constantly repeats the various motives introduced by the accompanying orchestra. Unfortunately, this musical concept lacks the spontaneous appeal that Mendelssohn's concerto immediately presents.

Mendelssohn's concerto was written in the 1800's and thus lends itself beautifully to the concept of subjectivity vs. the former objectivity which was vehemently stressed in earlier styles of music. Mendelssohn wrote five symphonies, one violin concerto, two piano concertos and two oratorios. Each has a unique distinction of its own, but all have the sensitivity and grace so embedded in the Romantic era.

The pieces of Beethoven, Mozart, Capuzzi, Bruch, Mendelssohn and Beriot were eloquently sequenced in the program which yielded a pleasant diversity to the concert. Each piece was artistically recaptured by the young musicians. The concertmaster's short interviews with each performer gave the concert a special touch of class which is somewhat devoid in similar youth concerts.

Montessori Grammar Symbols

Maria Montessori used the following symbols to help children recognized the names and functions of the different parts of speech. The following coloring code is still used in Montessori schools today.

Article	Small Gray Triangle
Noun	Black Equilateral Triangle
Adjective	Blue Equilateral Triangle
Pronoun	Pink Isocele
Verb	Red Circle
Adverb	Smaller Orange Circle
Conjunction	Purple/Mauve Bar
Preposition	Green Crescent
Interjection	Sunny Yellow Skittle Shape

The following game which I created to help my fourth, fifth, sixth and seventh graders recognize and understand the parts of speech, combines the bingo format with the Maria Montessori grammar symbol concept. I have found that children in the 9-12 age bracket enjoy bingo games. They find them to be both relaxing and educational way to learn new concepts.

EXAMPLE OF WORDS FOR
DIFFERENT PARTS OF SPEECH

Article	Noun	Pronoun
A	Girl	She
An	Boy	They
The	School	We
	Deer	He
	Table	I
	Bicycle	It
	Book	You

Adjective	Verb	Adverb
Pretty	Ran	Quietly
Two	Jump	Slowly
Few	Sit	Rarely
Blue	Were	Carefully
Short	Am	Here

Conjunction	Preposition	Interjection
And	On	Oh
Nor	Over	Wow
Or	In	Ah
But	Up	Ow

Since **Modern Montessori at Home** presents a complete introduction to the Montessori method of presenting the parts of speech, it is suggested that you borrow a copy at your library for review purposes.

For the Grammar Bingo Game you will need to purchase index or flash cards measuring 3" x 9" or 3" x 5", a multicolor packet of construction paper and lightweight posterboard measuring 9" x 12".

Directions

Using sheets of gray construction paper, encourage your child to cut small gray triangles. Explain to your child that these gray triangles will be used as markers for the bingo game. For example, explain that when he sees a word on his bingo card that represents an article i.e. like a, an or the he will place a gray triangle over that word. Next, using a black sheet of construction paper, instruct your child to cut out black equilateral triangles. Explain that these triangles will be used as markers for words that represent nouns. Your child will need to cut out several isoceles from a sheet of pink construction paper. Using red construction paper, your child should cut out several medium sized circles should be cut out of orange colored construction paper. Using

ARTICLE   PREPOSITION   INTERJECTION

CONJUNCTION   NOUN   VERB

ADJECTIVE   ADVERB   PRONOUN

138

a sheet of purple or mauve colored construction paper, ask your child to cut out several bar shapes; while sheets of green construction paper should be used to cut out crescent shapes. Finally, the interjection is represented by the skittle shape, and sunny yellow construction paper should be used to represent words like Oh!, Wow! and so on. Encourage your child to review page 138 of this book and pages 56 and 57 of **Modern Montessori at Home.**

Like the World Geography Bingo Game mentioned earlier in this book, the amount of cards you will need for Grammar Bingo will depend upon how many parts of speech you want to present in your game. Initially, I suggest presenting four parts of speech. Later, you will want to include additional parts of speech; consequently, you will need to include more game cards which represent the additional parts of speech introduced. For the first game, between 15-20 game cards will suffice. (See page 141).

First, take one of the 9" x 12" game cards and draw a line horizontally, dividing the area of the card in half. (As you will notice, the format of the cards for the Grammar Bingo Game is identical to the one used for the World Geography Game.) Next, draw two vertical lines so that the card is now divided into six equal squares. In each square you will write a different part of speech.

Make a master sheet which lists each of the parts of speech and examples of the parts of speech under the appropriate heading. (See pages 137-138 for a few examples.) Once you have completed writing the words you wish to include on your master list, you will be ready to enlist your child to help you transfer the words onto the cards.

Encourage your child to study the master list carefully. Undoubtedly, he is familiar with the various parts

139

of speech and the examples of words which are representative of nouns, pronouns, verbs, adverbs, conjunctions and the like. However, at this point, it is often useful to review the parts of speech with him. For example, you will want to review that the noun represents persons, places and things. The pronoun takes the place of a proper noun, i.e. **I, she, they** and the like. The adjective is a describing word. It makes a dull sentence come alive, while the verb is a word which may be either state of being or action. Examples of state of being verbs are **am, are, were** and **was,** while action verbs are represented by such words as **ran, hop, race,** etc. The adverb's function is to modify the verb. Examples like **quietly** and **lightly** can be used to modify the verb.

Examples like **quietly** and **lightly** can be used in sentences to stress this point. **The cat sat quietly.** Or **The girl lightly stroked the cat's fur.** Conjunctions like **and, or, nor, but,** and **for** join two sentences together. Prepositions like **in, around** and **over** may begin a prepositional phrase and have a noun as an object. Interjections alert the reader to emotions which are relevant to the sentence and story.

Now, ask your child if there are additional words that he wishes to include on the master sheet. If not, ask him to write words from the master sheet which represent the different parts of speech. Encourage him to select only two words per category per game card. For example, there are six squares on each game card; therefore, there should only be two words which are nouns, two words which are verbs, two words which represent adjectives and so on. (See page 141 for an example of how a finished game card might look.)

Notice that in this example, the top left hand square is occupied by the word **is** which is a state of being verb. In the middle, the word **in** which is a preposition appears. In the top right hand square the word **quietly** which is an adverb appears. In the bottom right hand corner square the verb **ran** appears. In the middle lower square the pronoun **she** is seen. Finally, the right lower square is occupied by the word **Oh!** which is an interjection.

Using the master list, suggest that your child produce 15 game cards for the game. So that the game will be more enlightening, advise that he use a word no more than once. If he makes 15 cards he will have 90 words to select from. Next, using about 20 index cards have him copy the parts of speech, one part of speech per card. Therefore, he will have several cards which read noun, several cards which state adjective, several cards which say conjunction and so on. Remind him to include all of the parts of speech. Now, the two of you are set to have some fun!

First, place the grammar shape symbols to one side. Next, shuffle the index and game cards. Ask your child to select a game card for you while he takes another one for himself. Now, place the index cards into a single pile. Draw the top card. Read the part of speech given. For example, if the card says **pronoun** both you and your child will search your card for words like **it, they, she, he** and the like. If one of you has a game card with a pronoun written on it, then a pink isocele marker, which was made from the pink construction paper, will be placed over the pronoun. Now, it is your child's turn to select a card. Let's assume that the word **noun** is written on this index card. Both of you will now search for persons, places or things on your game cards. If one and/or both of you has nouns on the game card then a black equilateral triangle will be placed over each noun seen. The game will continue until one of you has three across, either top or bottom row. The first person who gets three in a row wins the game!

Diagraming Sentences

Another stimulating exercise involves the diagraming of sentences. Beginning diagraming exercises are given in **Modern Montessori at Home**. Only a brief review will be presented here. You may want to have your child review these basic diagraming exercises before proceeding on the advanced exercises.

Basic Diagraming
Example of a simple sentence:
1. The little boy laughed.

a	the (article)	A	little (adjective)
N	boy (noun)	V	laughed (verb)

The little boy laughed.

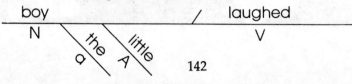

Example of a Simple Noun Verb Pattern
with compound adjective:

2. The beautiful but delicate vase shattered.

a   the (article)   A   beautiful (adjective)
C   but (coor. conj.)   A   delicate (adjective)
N   vase (noun)   V   shattered (verb)

The beautiful but delicate vase shattered.

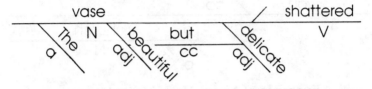

Example of Noun-Verb Pattern with Dual Adverb:

3. Gary goes there often.

N   Gary (noun)   V   goes (verb)
a   there (adverb)   a   often (adverb)

Gary goes there often.

Example of Noun-Verb Pattern with
Adverb Modifying another Adverb.

4. Carol learned very quickly.

N   Carol (noun)   V   learned (verb)
a   quickly (adverb)   a   very (adverb)

Carol learned very quickly.

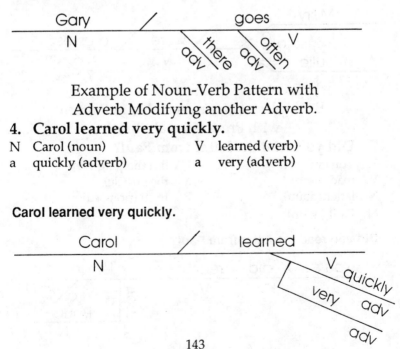

Example of Noun-Verb Pattern with
Prepositional Phrase acting as Adverb.

5. Go to the church.

S You (Subject understood) V go (verb)
P to (preposition) a the (article)
N church (noun)

Go to the church.

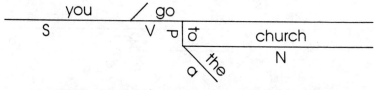

Example of Noun-Verb-Noun Pattern

6. Mary and Julie wore blue dresses.

N Mary (noun) cc and (coordinating conj.)
N Julie (noun) V wore (verb)
N dresses (noun) A blue (adjective)

Mary and Julie wore blue dresses.

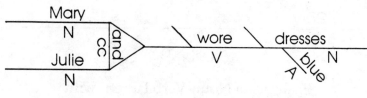

Examples of Noun-Verb-Noun Pattern
with Prepositional Phrase

7. Did you read the letter from Paul?

S You (subject) HV did (helping verb)
V read (verb) a the (article)
N letter (noun) P from (preposition)
N Paul (noun)

Did you read the letter from Paul?

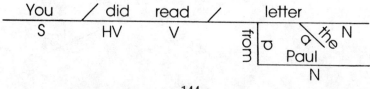

144

Example of an adjective clause introduced by a relative pronoun, i.e. who, whom

8. Mr. James, who is single, will marry Miss Woods.

N   Mr. James (noun)   HV will (helping verb)
V   marry (verb)   N   Miss Woods (noun)
RP who (relative pronoun)   V   is (verb)
A   single (adjective)

Mr. James, who is single, will marry Miss Woods.

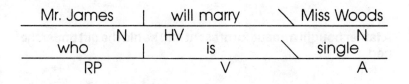

Diagraming a sentence with adverb phrase.

Explain to your child that when a prepositional phrase modifies a verb it becomes an adverb phrase.

9. In church, Judy and Mark reviewed the choral and instrumental music.

N   Judy (noun)   cc and (coordinating conj.)
N   Mark (noun)   V   reviewed (verb)
N   music (noun)   A   instrumental (adjective)
cc and (coordinating conj) A   choral (adjective)
P   in (preposition)   a   the (article)
n   church (object of prep. noun

In church, Judy and Mark reviewed the choral and instrumental music.

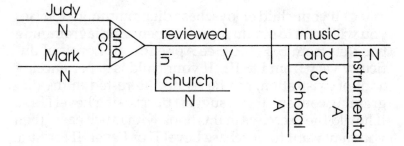

145

Compound sentence with adverb phrase.

10. A father bought a beautiful present and he hid the gift under the bed.

a	The (article)		N	father (noun)
V	bought (verb)		a	a (article)
A	beautiful (adjective)		N	present (noun)
cc	and (coordinating conj.)		P	he (pronoun)
V	hid (verb)		N	gift (noun)
P	under (preposition)		a	the (article)
N	bed (noun)			

A father bought a beautiful present and he hid the gift under the bed.

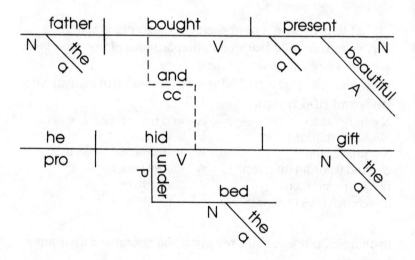

If your child enjoys these diagramming exercises you will want to obtain some inexpensive diagramming booklets from ESP, Inc. See Appendix B. Levels of difficulty vary from I to III. If your child is experienceing a lot of frustration, but he seems interested in the diagraming concept, then I suggest purchasing Level I first. If he did the exercises in this book with much ease, then you may want to purchase Level II or Level III for him.

BIBLIOGRAPHY

Montessori, Maria, The Absorbent Mind. New York, New York, The Dell Publishing Company, Inc., 1967.

Montessori, Maria, The Discovery of the Child. New York, New York Ballatine Books, 1986.

Montessori, Maria, Dr. Montessori's Own Handbook. New York, New York. Schoken Books, 1965.

Montessori, Maria, Education and Peace, Chicago, Illinois. Henry Regenery Company, 1972.

Montessori, Maria, From Childhood to Adolescence. New York, New York. Schoken Books, 1973.

Montessori, Maria, The Montessori Method. Cambridge, MA. Robert Bentley, Inc. 1965.

Montessori, Maria, The Secret of Childhood. New York, New York. Ballatine Books, 1986.

Montessori, Maria, Spontaneous Activity in Education. Cambridge, Massachusetts Robert Bentley, Inc., 1965.

APPENDIX A
Publishers of Recommended Books

A BEKA BOOKS
118 St. John Street, Pensacola, FL 32523-9160

EARLY WORK LEARNING TOOLS
P.O. Box 5635, Petaluma, CA 94953-5635

ESP, INC. Publishers of Super Workbooks
1201 E. Johnson Avenue, Jonesboro, AR 72403-5080

LADYBIRD BOOKS, INC.
49 Omni Circle, P.O. Box 1690, Auburn, ME 04210

LAKESHORE CURRICULUM MATERIALS
COMPANY
2695 E. Dominguez Street, Carson, CA 90740

PENDULUM PRESS, INC.
237 Saw Mill Road, West Haven, CT 06516

APPENDIX B
Selected Books for Children 10 through 12 Years of Age

The following books are published by:

A BEKA BOOKS
118 St. John Street, Pensacola, FL 32523-9160

Investigating God's World	(Science - 5th Grade Level)
Of America	(Reading - 5th Grade Level)
Old World History & Geography	(Soc. Science - 5th Grade Level)
Of America II	(Reading - 6th Grade Level)
Observing God's World	(Science - 6th Grade Level)
New World History & Geography	(Soc. Scinece - 6th Grade Level)
Grammar & Composition	(English - 7th Grade Level)
Of People	(Reading - 7th Grade Level)
Science: Order and Realty	(Science - 7th Grade Level)
Since the Beginning	(History - 7th Grade Level)

Addison, Anthony. 1989. The Children's Book of Questions and Answers. Treasure Press, Michelin House, 81 Fulhamm Rd, London SW3 6RB England

(4th Grade Level)

Boase, Wendy. 1978. Ancient Egypt. Glouster, New York

(5th Grade Level)

Cobb, Vicki. 1985. Chemically Active. J.B. Lippincott, New York.

(5th Grade Level)

Curzio, C. and Borelli, A. 1986. Simon and Schuster's Gems and Precious Stones. Simon & Schuster, New York.

(7th Grade Level)

Desautels, P.E. 1974. Collector's Series: Rocks & Minerals. Grosset & Dunlap Publishers, New York.   (7th Grade Level)

The following books are published by:

ESP, INC. Publishers of Super Workbooks
1201 E. Johnson Avenue, Jonesboro, AR 72403-5080

APPENDIX B
Continued

Government - Workbook   (7th Grade Level)
World Neighbors - Workbook   (5th–9th Grade Level)
Diagramming I - Workbook   (5th–9th Grade Level)
Diagramming II - Workbook   (5th–9th Grade Level)
Diagramming III - Workbook   (5th–9th Grade Level)

Gardner, Robert. 1982. Kitchen Chemistry. Julian Messner,
    New York.   (5th Grade Level)

Lauber, Patricia. 1989. Meteors and Meteorites: Voyagers from
    Space. Thomas Y. Crowell, New York.   (5th Grade Level)

Mebane, Robert C. and Rybolt,Thomas R. 1985. Adventures
    with Atoms and Molecules. Enslow Publishers, Inc., Hillside
                            (5th Grade Level)

Mitchell, R.S. 1985. Dictionary of Rocks. Van Nostrand
    Reinhold, New York.   (7th Grade Level.

Morgan, Alfred. 1962. First Chemistry Book for Boys and Girls.
    Charles Scribner's Sons, New York   (5th Grade Level)

Sorrell, C.A. 1973. A Guide to Field Identification of Rocks &
    Minerals. Golden Press, New York   (5th Grade Level)

Steere, Susan, and Ring, Kathryn. 1988. The Reef & The Wrasse.
    Harbinger House, Inc., 3131 N. Country Club, Tucson, AZ
    85716.   (4th Grade Level)

Stokes, Donald and Stokes, Lillian. 1989. The Hummingbird
    Book - The Complete Guide to Attracting, Identifying and
    Enjoying Hummingbirds. Little, Brown, Boston
                            (7th Grade Level)

APPENDIX B
Continued

The following books are published by:

THE YOUNG DISCOVERY LIBRARY
217 Main Street, Ossining, NY 10562, (800) 343-7854

On the Banks of Pharaoh's Nile
Living in Ancient Rome
Japan: Land of Samurai
Living in India
Australia
Cathedrals: Stone Upon Stone
Music! (instruments/orchestras)
TV and Films (*New)

Woods, G. 1988. Science in Ancient Egypt. Franklin Watts,
    New York.   (6th Grade Level)

APPENDIX C
Highly Recommended Resources for Parents and Teachers

A BEKA BOOKS
118 St. John Street, Pensacola, FL 32523-9160

CHRISTIAN HOME & SCHOOL MAGAZINE
3350 East Paris Avenue, P.O. Box 8709,
Grand Rapids, MI 49518-8709

ESP, INC. - Publishers of Super Workbooks
1201 E. Johnson Avenue, Jonesboro, AR 72403-5080

HOME EDUCATION PRESS - 1990 Homeschool Handbook
(Annually updated - excellent resource)
P.O. Box 1083, Tonasket, WA 98855 (509) 486-1351

HOME EDUCATION PRESS - Home Education Magazine
(Superb bimonthly magazine)
P.O. Box 1083, Tonasket, WA 98855 (509) 486-1351

IN-PRINT FOR CHILDREN
2113 Kenmore Avenue, Glenside, PA 94022

THE MAIL ORDER SHOPPER FOR PARENTS:
How to Get the Very Best for Your Children
from Infants to Teens
Published by Doubleday, a div. of Bantam Doubleday -
Dell Publishing Group, Inc.
Fifth Avenue, New York, NY 10103

MICHAEL OLAF: The Montessori Shop
P.O. Box 1162, 1101 "H" Street, Arcata, CA 95521 (707) 826-1557

MONTESSORI COURIER MAGAZINE -
Pubished by the London Montessori Centre
18 Balderton Street, London, WIY ITG England

MONTESSORI LIFE MAGAZINE -
A Publication of The American Montessori Society
150 Fifth Avenue, New York, NY 10011-4384

APPENDIX D
Books and Publications Recommended for Lesson Planning

Beck, Barbara. 1983. The Ancient Maya. Franklin Watts, NY.

EDMUND SCIENTIFIC
101 E. Gloucester Pike, Barrington, NJ 08007

EDUCATIONAL RECORD CENTER, INC.
Bldg. 400, Suite 400, 1575 Northside Dr., N.W.
Atlanta, GA 30318

ELDERLY INSTRUMENTS
1100 N. Washington, P.O. Box 14210, Lansing, MI 48901

FAMILY TRAVEL TIMES
TRAVEL WITH YOUR CHILDREN
80 Eighth Ave, New York, NY 10011

HANSEN PLANETARIUM PUBLICATIONS
1098 S. 200 W., Salt Lake City, UT 84101

HOBBY CITY
American Indian Store
Rock & Gem Shop
1238 S. Beach Blvd., Anaheim, CA 92804

MacEachern, Diane. 1990. SAVE OUR PLANET: 750 Everyday
Ways You Can Help Clean Up the Earth. Dell, New York.

McLeish, Kenneth & McLeish, Valerie. 1986. Listener's Guide to
Classical Music. Longman Group Limited, Longman
House, Burnt Mill, Harlow Essex CM20 27E England

THE METROPOLITAN MUSEUM OF ART
Special Service Office, Middle Village, NY 11381

Meyer, Carolyn & Gallenkamp, Charles. 1985. The Mystery of
the Anicent Maya. Atheneum, New York.

NATIONAL GALLERY OF ART
Publications Office, Washington, D.C. 20565

APPENDIX D
Continued

Rattner, David. 1976. Enjoying the Arts/Music. Richards Rosen Press, Inc. NY

Seay, Albert. 1965. Music in the Medieval World. Prentice-Hall, Englewood Cliffs.

Sherwood, Martin. 1985. CHEMISTRY TODAY: The World Book Encyclopedia of Science. World Book, Inc., Chicago.

Van Duryn, Jane. 1980. Builders on the Desert. Julian Messner, New York.

Wilson, John. 1980. The Complete Works of William Shakespeare. Octupus Books Limited, London. Distributed by Mayflower Books, Inc., 575 Lexington Ave., New York, NY 10022.

APPENDIX E
Films and Cassettes Recommended for Lesson Planning

ANIMALS, ANIMALS! (Look, Listen, Explore) National
 Geographic Society Educational Services, Dept. 90,
 Washington, D.C. 20036. 1990.
 2 filmstrips, 2 guides, 2 cassettes.

The following books are published by:

ESP, INC. Publishers of Super Workbooks
1201 E. Johnson Avenue, Jonesboro, AR 72403-5080

Pollution & Our Environment	(Recommended for Grades 3-6)
Energy & Man	(Recommended for Grades 3-6)
The Healthy Body	(Recommended for Grades 3-6)
Energy & Man	(Recommended for Grades 3-6)
Using the Library	(Recommended for Grades 4-8)

EXPLORING ENVIRONMENTS:
Australian Broadcasting Corp., Landmark Films
 3450 Slade Run Dr., Falls Church, VA 22042. 1989.
 (2 programs)
 At Home in the Rainforest
 At Home on the Barrier Reef

EXPLORING TIDEPOOLS. Sunburst Communications,
 39 Washington Ave., Pleasantville, NY 10570. 1989.
 (Apple II Series - 128K color monitor, mouse and printer).
 2 disks, guide and backups.

JEWISH TALES FROM THE HEART. Tales for the Telling,
 99 Arlington St., Brighton, MA 02135. 1989.
 40 min. cassette.

A JOURNEY THROUGH HANUKKAH. Audio Pathways
 Family Series, 186 Castle Blvd., Akron, OH 44313 90 min.
 3 cassettes, paperback.

APPENDIX E
Continued

THE PHARAOHS. Coronet Film & Video, 108 Wilmot Road, Deerfield, IL 60015. 1989.

SUCCESS WITH LITERATURE: Romeo and Juliet. Scholastic, P.O. Box 7502, Jefferson City, MO 65102. 1989. (Apple II series - 128K and printer) 2 disks, guide and student's guide.

INDEX

INDEX (Cont.)

To order additional copies of:

MODERN MONTESSORI AT HOME II:
A Creative Teaching Guide for Parents of
Children 10 through 12 Years of Age

MODERN MONTESSORI AT HOME:
A Creative Teaching Guide for Parents of
Children Six through Nine Years of Age

MONTESSORI AT HOME:
A Complete Guide to Teaching Your Preschooler
at Home Using the Montessori Method

Send $9.95 each plus $1.50 shipping per book to:

American Montessori Consulting
P.O. Box 5062,
Rossmoor, CA 90721-5062